The Northern Echo

North Country Golf

By Adrian Green and Tim Wellock

The Authors

ADRIAN GREEN has been playing golf for 22 years, and has maintained a handicap of one or scratch for the past 17. He was selected for the England Schoolboys while a student at Queen Elizabeth Sixth Form College, Darlington. During his 80 plus appearances for Durham County he has become familiar with many courses in the North-East. This prompted him to take on the novel challenge of playing one hole on all 38 courses in Durham on the longest day of 1991. He has written a golfing column for The Northern Echo since the early nineties first Through the Green and more recently Club Call.

TIM WELLOCK, formerly The Northern Echo's deputy sports editor, has worked as a freelance sports writer and sub-editor since 1988. A member of Barnard Castle Golf Club, he now concentrates on covering Durham's first-class cricket matches, but was the Echo's golf correspondent from 1988-91, when he recommended Adrian Green as his successor. Together they helped to fill in the long winter months by putting together the articles which form the basis of this book.

Symbols used in this book

18 holes

36 holes

9 holes

Parkland course

Moorland course

Links course

Clubs for hire

Buggy hire

Pro shop

Driving range

Restaurant

Bar

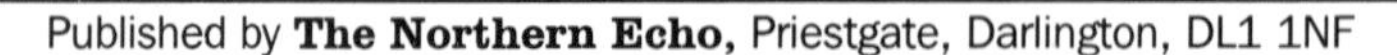
Published by **The Northern Echo,** Priestgate, Darlington, DL1 1NF

North Country Golf

Contents

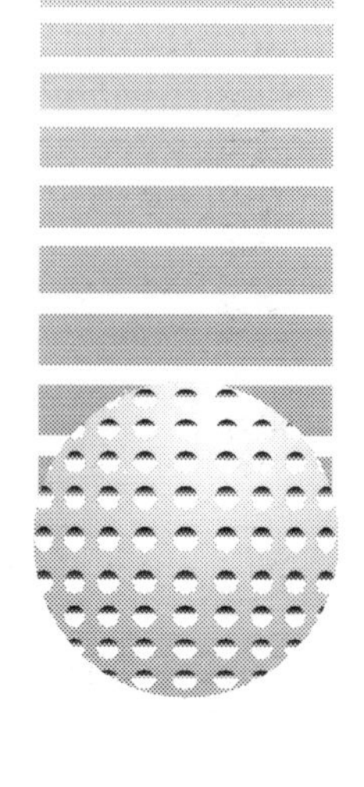

Foreword

As I referred to in my recent book, Botham, My Autobiography, my sporting aspirations may well have been different if at an early age I had been handed a seven iron as opposed to a cricket bat, bearing in mind how I feel about golf today!

I discovered the beauty of the Royal and Ancient game while still pursuing my cricketing career and since retiring from the crease in 1993 I have endeavoured to make up for lost time on the links and in so doing reduced my handicap to a respectable five at the time of going to press.

Having been resident in the North-East for a number of years I have been fortunate enough to sample some of the wonderful courses available in this neck of the woods, my personal favourite being the magnificent champsionship course near Hexham, Slaley Hall.

Other courses of which I am extremely fond are Seaton Carew, Brancepeth Castle and my home club Darlington, which is always in good condition for most of the year.

I have known Adrian Green since joining Darlington some years ago and I am familiar with his Club Call articles which translate the passion which he has for the game, especially in his adopted North-East.

I have enjoyed discovering the many relatively hidden golfing treasures which this part of the country has in store. I am sure that with this book as a guide, you will too.

Ian Botham

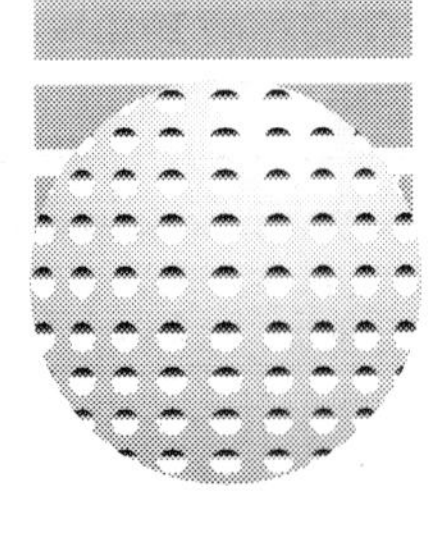

Introduction

MUCH of the work which has gone into the compilation of this book was initially inspired by the fact that the North-East is widely observed to be a golfing backwater.

The list of the top 50 courses in the British Isles, as published in Golf World magazine in November, 1992, shows the North of England as a vast golfing desert.

Ganton, near Scarborough, is the only course included north of Alwoodley, on the outskirts of Leeds.

In a series of articles published in The Northern Echo under the title of Clubcall, we set out to show that there are some superb courses in our region.

We also looked beyond the best courses, such as Seaton Carew, Brancepeth and Slaley Hall, to find those which have something special to offer; whether it be the history of Alnmouth or Cleveland; the views of Consett or Catterick; the team and individual honours won by Teesside, Hartlepool and Darlington; or the sheer all-round excellence of Bishop Auckland and Wearside.

We have also looked at some of the region's newest creations, of which some are by no means outstanding courses but all have an interesting story to tell.

At the time of going to press, there are, of course, several more courses under construction, notably at the Ramside Hall Hotel near Durham City and at Wynyard Hall, the Wolviston home of Sir John Hall.

In Northumberland a 27-hole complex is coming on stream at Burgham Hall, just south of Felton on the A1, and there are also very high hopes for Matfen Hall, north of Corbridge, while the well-established little course at Alnwick is expanding to 18 holes.

Generally we received marvellous hospitality wherever we went, and were left with the very strong impression that a lot of people are working hard to ensure that good golf is accessible to as many people as possible in the North-East.

Tim Wellock

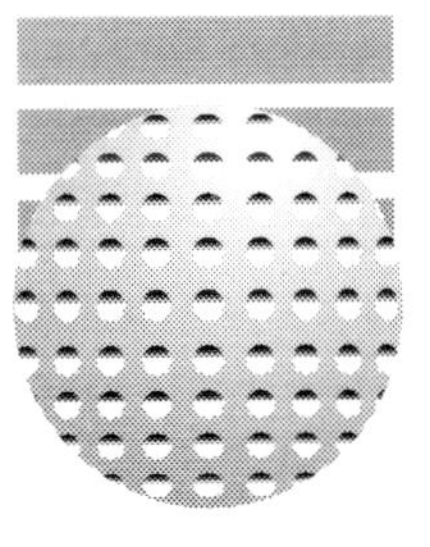

NORTHUMBERLAND

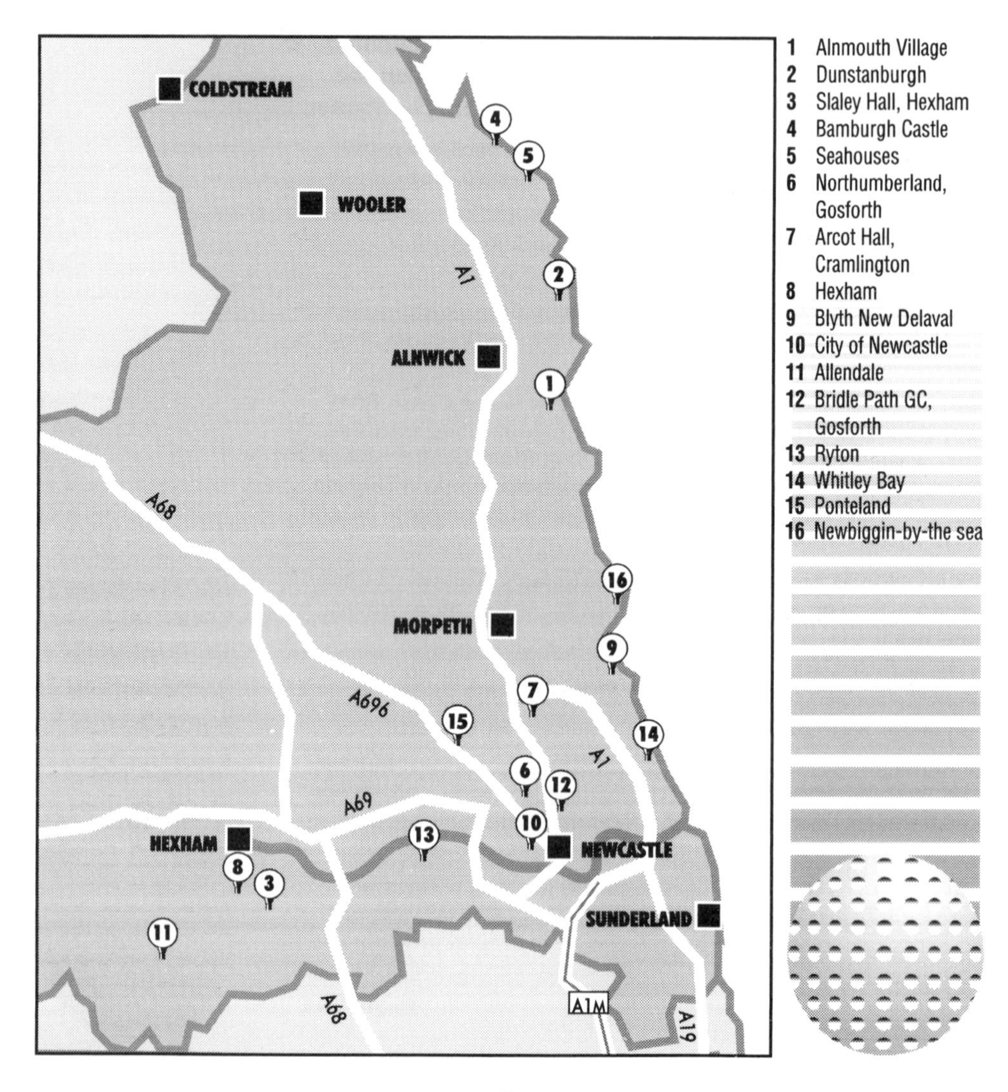

Northumberland courses

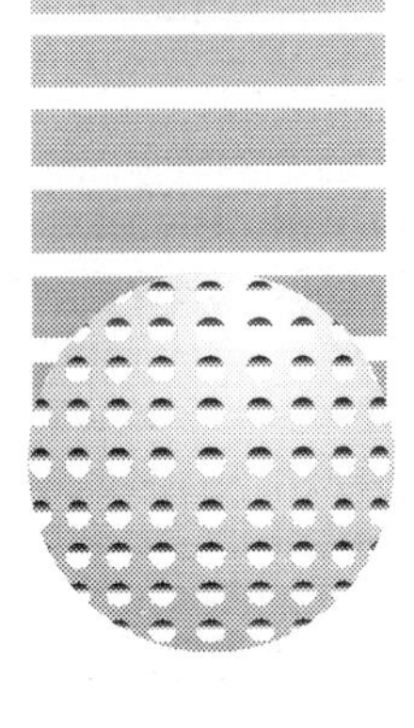

Alnmouth Village Golf Club

ANY history of golf in Northumberland must begin at Alnmouth. Although the Alnmouth club is now at Foxton Hall, a mile north of the village, it began life in 1869 on a narrow strip of links land where the holes have changed little to this day.

The club now occupying this nine-hole site is known as Alnmouth Village, and although the delightful little clubhouse now stages bingo evenings, it's here where the real feel of golf in the early days lives on.

Alnmouth and Royal Liverpool (Hoylake) share the honour of being the fourth oldest clubs in England after Blackheath, Westward Ho and Royal Wimbledon.

A book on the history of golf at Alnmouth, by Deryck Walton and Jack Steedman, outlines how, in August 1869, Capt Arthur Walker issued a notice to likely members of his intention to create a golf club.

The first AGM was held on October 19 that same year in the Schooner Inn.

The course is believed to have been designed by the 1874 Open champion Mungo Park, who became the club's first professional/greenkeeper. He and his brother Willie Park junior, another Open champion, took part in the club's first professional tournament in 1881.

Three years later the clubhouse was built on the site it still occupies, the ground being donated by J W Pease, who apparently stipulated that it must never be used for any other purpose.

The course was extended to 18 holes in 1905, moving up the hill from the strip of land between the sea and the old cliffline.

The new course was opened by the Duke of Northumberland and a match between Harry Vardon and J H Taylor marked the occasion.

Problems with erosion began as early as the 1920s and it is recorded that £3,000 was spent on sea defence from 1922-27.

In 1928 people with property overlooking the course were apparently told that the value of their homes depended entirely on the golf course and they were persuaded to come up with a further £600 for sea defence measures.

But by this time the seeds of discontent had already been sown, which eventually forced the split in the club.

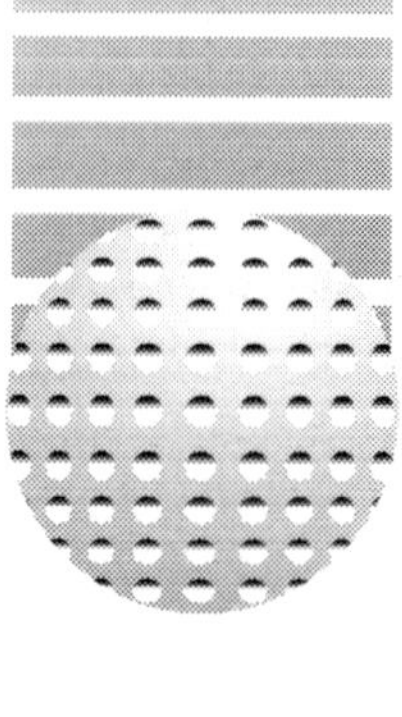

View down the 1st hole from Alnmouth Village clubhouse

In the early days there was an agreement between the Burgesses of Alnmouth and the villagers allowing the locals to play on the course without contributing to its upkeep, and it was reported in the Press that 'it was quite a natural thing to see plus fours playing with fishing jerseys.'

However, the fact that the course was on common land, where stint holders were permitted to graze cattle, was not to everyone's liking.

The arrival of charabancs after the war, disgorging trippers with their picnics on to the greens, was said to be the final straw.

In the mid-1920s a committee approached the Duke of Northumberland, who agreed to release more land around Foxton Hall, a historic residence of the Percy family.

Money was raised through £25 debentures, for which 50 members applied, and in 1929 Harry Colt designed the new course, incorporating nine holes from the old one.

The exisiting club was dissolved and a new club was formed on January 1, 1930. The split was complete when the Alnmouth Village club was formed in 1936 to take over and run the original nine holes on the old

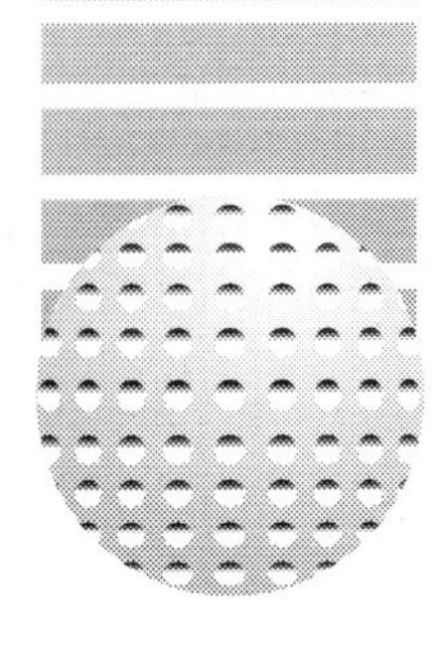

Alnmouth Village Golf Club

links. The subscription was one guinea.

Foxton went from strength to strength with Eddie Fernie continuing as professional for 39 years.

The son of Willie Fernie of Troon, the Open champion in 1883, he had taken over from local man George Rochester in 1924.

Rochester had succeeded Mungo Park in 1889 and when Fernie retired in 1964 the club had had only three professionals.

David Fletcher followed Fernie and his daughter Linzi is one of two Curtis Cup players produced by the club, the other being Margaret Pickard, who was English champion in 1960 and runner-up in 1967.

There have also been two internationals among the men in Keith Tate and Peter Deeble, who was the English amateur champion in 1980.

The old divisions between the two clubs evidently remain today, with the Village people giving the impression that they regard the Foxton folk up the hill as the snobs of the parish.

Serious golfers inevitably head for Foxton, but the village course retains a modest charm and is not without its highlights.

FACTFILE

Address: Alnmouth Village Golf Club, Marine Road, Alnmouth, Northumberland

Telephone: (01665) 830370

How to get there: From Alnwick on A1 to Alnmouth on A1068

Green Fees: Weekdays £10; weekends £20

Course length: 6,414 yards

SSS: 71

Other information: Catering can be arranged for parties with the club.

The first five holes head out through the humps and hollows, with the beach on the right all the way, then the sixth involves a drive up on to the clifftop.

A marker post gives the best line, and once you have climbed the steep path you realise there's still quite an ascent to the green, with Foxton's fairways over the fence to the right.

It is reported that when Tony Jacklin once played at Foxton he climbed the fence here to admire the view from the Village club's seventh tee. Once there, it is not difficult to see why.

This most elevated of tee shots takes you back down the cliff for the final three holes of the first circuit.

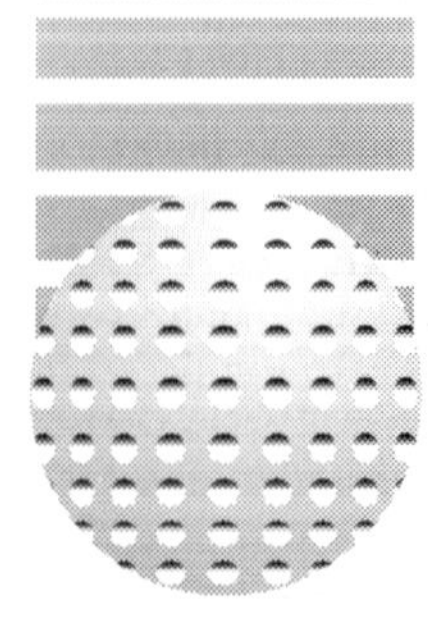

Dunstanburgh Castle Golf Club

TIME almost stands still on the enchanting golf course which has graced Embleton links since 1900. But not quite.

With a First World War Nissen hut as its clubhouse, Dunstanburgh Castle, one of the unsung gems of the Northumberland coast, has always been the sort of place where you feel metal woods ought to be banned. Hickory shafts would be more appropriate.

Changes are afoot but nothing too extensive, and certainly not visually intrusive, because this is National Trust land and everything about it is well worth preserving.

The hut has gone, giving way to a new clubhouse. Other concessions to modern methods include consultation with the Sports Turf Research Institute at Bingley in order to improve the greens.

Otherwise time stands as still as the bewitching ruins of the 14th-century castle itself. Little can be done, for example, about the rabbit scrapes which litter the fourth and fifth fairways. Poisons cannot be used because the famous Craster to Beadnell walk follows the seaward edge of the course.

If you're the sort of golfer who likes his fairways perfectly manicured, this is not the place for you. But if you appreciate the pleasures of playing on a site of outstanding beauty, you will find nothing more rewarding in the North-East.

There is only one par five, quite a challenge at 537 yards but six of the par fours are over 400 yards and the course would measure more than its 6,298 yards but for the fact that two of its par threes barely top 100 yards.

The feature hole, the 13th, is also the shortest, a 105-yard flick over a rocky sea inlet, which can have even the bravest quaking in their golf shoes if the wind is blowing.

From here on in, arable fields provide an unattractive out of bounds down the left, but they are all testing holes, especially the 18th.

At 444 yards it has a tidal burn some 20 yards short of the green, laying down a challenge to those hoping to get home in the regulation two strokes.

The first is a similar distance and is followed by a short, sharp climb to an elevated section of the course flanked by dunes dotted with holiday chalets.

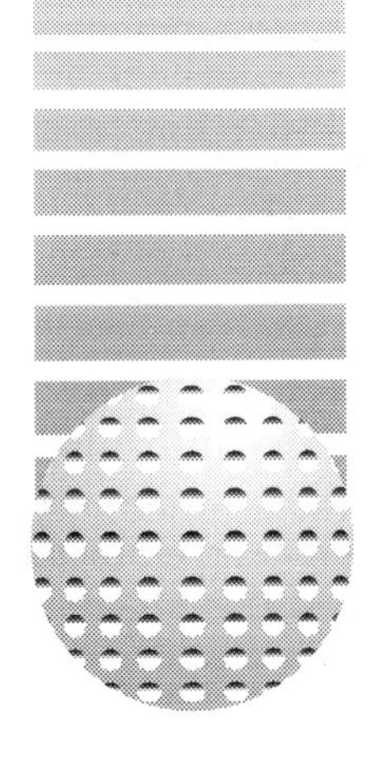

Dunstanburgh Castle Golf Club

The 13th at Dunstanburgh Castle

The third is a lovely dog-leg left, where the big hitter might try to nip off the corner. If he fails the gorse which abounds on this part of the course will ensure he never sees his ball again.

The fourth is a 166-yard par three to a plateau green and the sixth is a magnificent hole, teeing off from the top of the path leading up the hill from the first green.

With the rest of the course visible ahead from this superb vantage point, this tee shot offers another daunting challenge as the hole sweeps left around the bay.

The seventh and eighth are true links holes in among the dunes, while nine ten and 12 are all very good long par fours heading towards the castle. The 11th green is one of those which has had to be relaid,

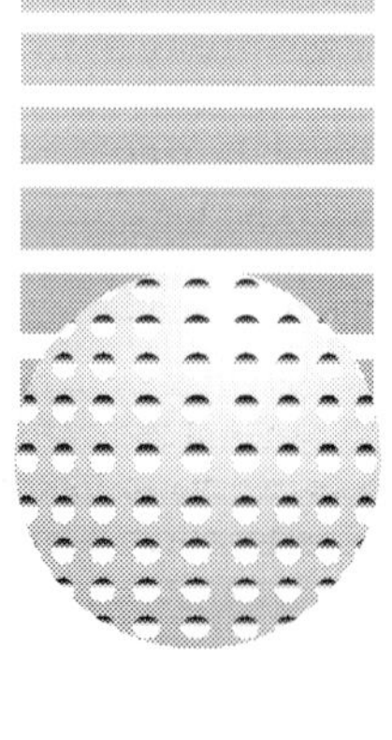

having suffered badly during several years of drought.

The club's owner, Peter Gilbert, leases the course from the National Trust and splits his time between running the club and working as a neuro physiologist at University College in London. He says this is a labour of love.

'I was brought up in Newcastle and my parents had a house near the course,' he said. 'I took over the lease six years ago and recently signed a longer lease with the National Trust.

'I have a very detailed environmental conservation agreement with them, which insists that I protect the flora and fauna.'

Gilbert's research has shown that the course was laid out in 1900 by Dunstanburgh Castle estate staff as a nine-hole course for guests of a hotel.

Just after the war the course was bought by Sir Arthur Munro-Sutherland, who brought in James Braid to design the layout still in use today.

He did his job well, as have those who followed. This course remains an absolute joy.

FACTFILE

Address: Dunstanburgh Castle Golf Club, Embleton, Alnwick, Northumberland.

Telephone: (01665) 576562

How to get there: Eight miles north east of Alnwick off the A1

Course length: 6,298

Green Fees: Weekdays £12.50; weekends £16

SSS: 70

Other information: Society playing rates, catering rates, by arrangement with club.

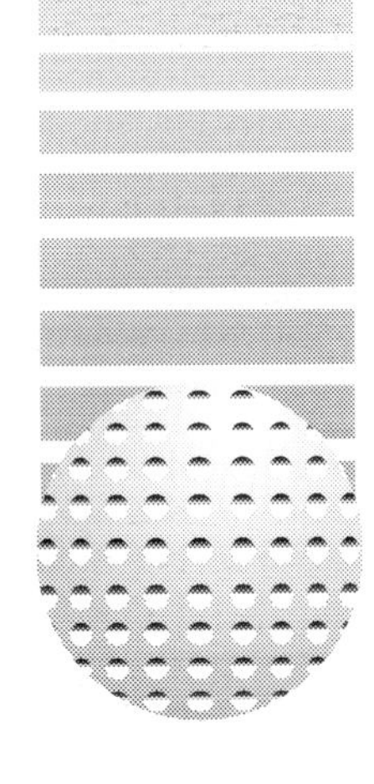

Slaley Hall Golf Club

WHEN Christy O'Connor Jnr was proudly presented as Slaley Hall's touring professional in 1990, the publicity material described the complex as 'the ultimate dream'.

Twenty months later it went into receivership, leaving holiday villas, barely-used timeshare lodges and what was to have been a 140-room five-star hotel standing as stark reminders of how the dream almost turned to dust.

The course was already being hailed as potentially among the finest in Europe when the banks pulled the plug in September 1991.

As it was Friday the 13th, the date remained etched in the memory of Stuart Brown, Golf Director at the 340-acre complex five miles south of Hexham. But he remains utterly convinced that the dream will be realised, largely because of a chance meeting.

'When the development went bust we were very worried about the course and I went to a greenkeepers' show at Harogate. I bumped into someone I had met in a tournament at Woburn in 1986, when he was a rep with ICI. It turned out he was now managing director of ICI Chemical Products, so I told him about our problems and he came up to see the course. They took samples from the whole course and found it was totally dead. It was simply under-nourished and was in danger of going to seed.

'They decided to use the course as a flagship to show what their products can achieve. '

Despite the problems, Brown was able to keep the golf club running as a going concern, with 200 members paying £325 and visitors paying green fees of £22.50. There are a further 200 on a waiting list, but Brown feels that restricting the membership did help to ensure the course has not been overplayed.

'I have played all over the world and this is the finest estate course I have seen. The European Tour decided when the course was only a year old that they wanted to bring the English Open here.'

The complex was said to be about six weeks from completion when it went into receivership, and the official estimate of the debt was £27m. It had been the brainchild of Tyneside financier Seamus O'Carroll, who bought the site in 1984 for £1m.

He brought in former Ryder Cup player Dave Thomas to design the course and it was conceived with a major tournament in mind, with mounding to accommodate 35,000 spectators. The combination of

Sun dial at the rear of the 18th green at Slaley Hall

woodland and moorland provided the opportunity to create a rich variety of holes, while the gorse and rhododendrons added natural colour. Some of the water features which have been created might look a little unnatural for some tastes, but the overall achievement is a course of beauty and difficulty.

The ninth hole could come to be known as one of the finest in Europe. Tree-lined and with a stream cascading down the uphill part of the fairway, it looks stunning, and it is also fiendishly difficult. It is the stroke index one hole, being a par four which plays longer than its 452 yards because the second shot is uphill to a two-tier green.

Woe betide anyone who hits his approach to the top tier when the flag is on the front, because Slaley's

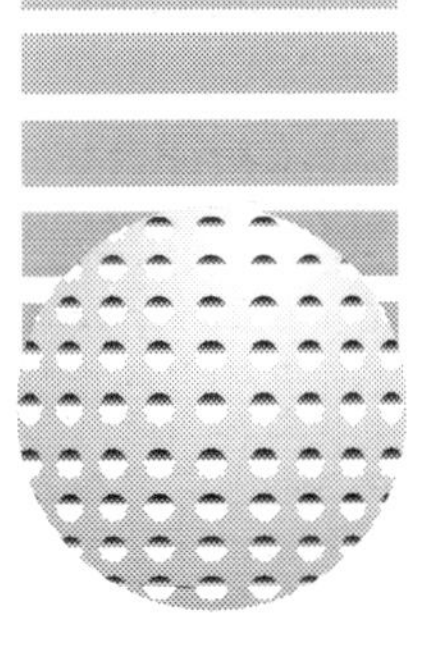

Slaley Hall Golf Club

sand-based greens are lightning fast.

The 18th, a 460 yard par four, is another magnificent hole, featuring a tight drive before the long approach is struck across a valley to the green in front of the stately old hall, which will eventually form part of the hotel.

There are only three par threes on the par 72 course, of which the most difficult is the sixth, 205 yards off the back tee across a lake to a green set in trees.

The second hole is a classic dog leg where if the ball is not struck past the angle of the corner off the tee the ultimate price of laying up may be the only option. There is enough room to create a second 18 holes, which Brown is convinced will go ahead, along with all the other facilities originally planned. The timeshare lodges, in sylvan lakeside settings, provide the last word in luxury, and even in receivership they won a gold award from RCI Europe, who organise timeshare exchange.

The clubhouse will eventually be situated in the hotel complex, which will also include a golf academy and a leisure club with swimming pools, spas, saunas, solaria and a gymnasium. The first nine holes were opened in 1989 and the full course the following year, with the whole development originally scheduled for completion in August 1990. Work fell further and further behind until receivers Touche Ross were called in. They were later replaced by Arthur Anderson who at the time of going to press looked as near as ever to completing the sale. Fourteen staff were retained, of which six were green staff who ensured that the course was brought into first class condition and applied finishing touches such as transplanting a lot of Scotch pine.

Says Brown: 'We want to create a golf club which surpasses any other. It has to be spot on for the membership, whether they be individual, family, corporate or overseas members.'

FACTFILE

Address: Slaley Hall Golf Club, Slaley, Hexham, Norethumberland.

Telephone: (01434) 673350

How to get there: Off A68 near Corbridge

Green Fees: Weekdays £30 for round £40 for day; weekends £30 – bookings only.

Course length: 7,038

Par: 72

Other information: Driving range and practice ground.

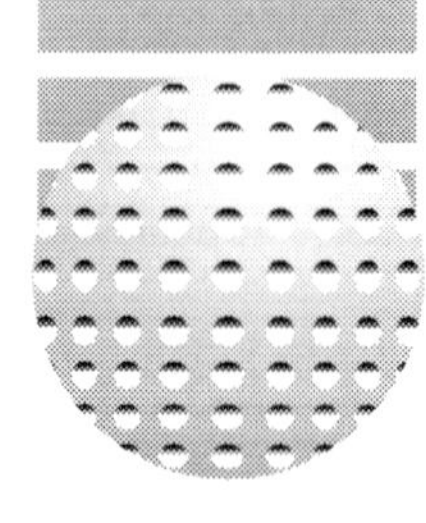

A golfer crosses the bridge at Slaley Hall Golf Club.

South Shields golf course.

City of Newcastle

Address: Three Mile Bridge, Gosforth, Newcastle upon Tyne, NE3 2DR
Telephone: (0191) 285 1775
How to get there: Three miles north of the city centre on the A1. Opposite the Three Mile Inn.
Course: Parkland, 18 holes, 6,508 yards
SSS: 71
Special features: Designed by Harry Vardon
Founded: 1892
Visitors: Welcome except on men's competition days
Green fees: £19 week days, £21 weekends and Bank Holidays.
Hotels: Gosforth Park
Further information: Lunches, bar snacks and sandwiches every day except Mondays. Snooker and pool

Blyth

Address: New Delaval and Newsham, Blyth, Northumberland, NE24 4DB
Telephone: (01670) 367728
How to get there: Eleven miles north of Newxastle, six miles North of Whitley Bay.
Course: Parkland, 18 holes, 6,533 yards
SSS :72
Special features: Designed by Hamilton Stutt and Co.
Founded: 1905
Visitors: Welcome weekdays only, before 3pm unless with a club member.
Green fees: £16 per round, £18 per day – £6 with playing member.
Special packages: Societieds welcome by previous arrangement. Please give 28 days advance notice.
Further information: Full catering facilities.

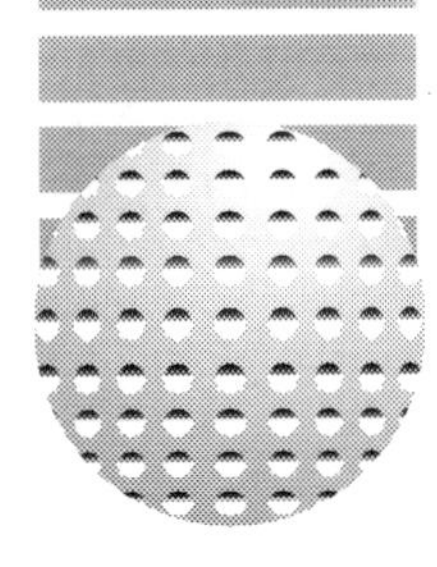

Gosforth Bridle Path

Address: Broadway East, Gosforth, Newcastle upon Tyne, NE3 5ER
Telephone: (1091) 285 3495
How to get there: Course is three miles north out of the city centre. Turn right at the first main roundabout after Regent Street Centre metro station.
Course: Meadowland, 18 holes, 6,043 yards
SSS: 69
Founded: 1905
Visitors: Welcome on weekdays, members' guests only before 4pm weekends and on Bank Holidays.
Green fees: £18 WD.
Special packages: Societies welcome weekdays.
Hotels: Gosforth Park.
Further information: Full catering facilities except Mondays.

Hexham

Address: Spital Park, Hexham, Northumberland, NE46 3RZ
Telephone: (01434) 603072
How to get there: One mile west of Hexham town centre on the A69
Course: Parkland, 18 holes, 6,026 yards
SSS: 68
Special features: Designed by Harry Vardon
Founded: 1907
Visitors: Welcome any day
Green fees: £20 per round, £26 per day
Special packages: Societies welcome by arrangement, not Saturdays and Sundays
Hotels: Beaumont, Royal
Further information: Full catering facilities every day

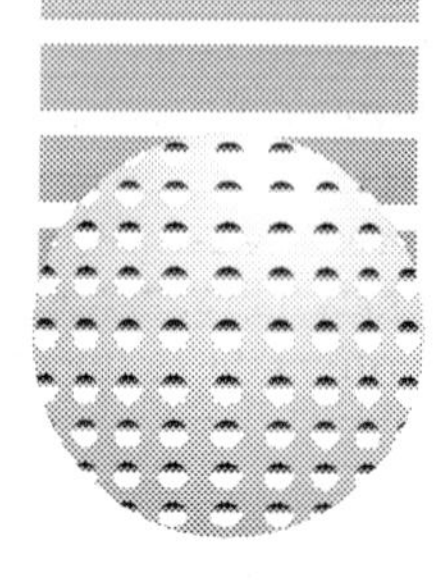

Ponteland

Address: 53 Bell Villas, Ponteland, Newcastle upon Tyne NE20 9BD
Telephone: (01661) 2689
How to get there: One and a half miles north of Newcastle airport on the A696 Jedburgh road
Course: Parkland, 18 holes, 6,512 yards
SSS: 71
Special features: Designed by Harry Ferney
Founded: 1927
Visitors: Welcome Monday to Friday
Green fees: £22.50 per day
Special packages: Societies welcome Tuesday and Thursdays
Further information: Full catering during bar hours, at other times by prior arrangement

Whitley Bay

Address: Claremont Road, Whitley bay, Tyne and Wear, NE26 3UF
Telephone: (0191) 252 0180
How to get there: Course situated at north end of town, ten miles north east of Newcastle on the A183
Course: Links and parkland, 18 holes, 6,617 yards
SSS: 72
Founded: 1890
Visitors: Welcome except at weekends
Green fees: £18 per round, £25 per day
Special packages: Societies welcome weekdays by arrangement
Hotels: Gosforth Park, Holiday Inn, Windsor
Further information: Full bar and restaurant facilities except Mondays

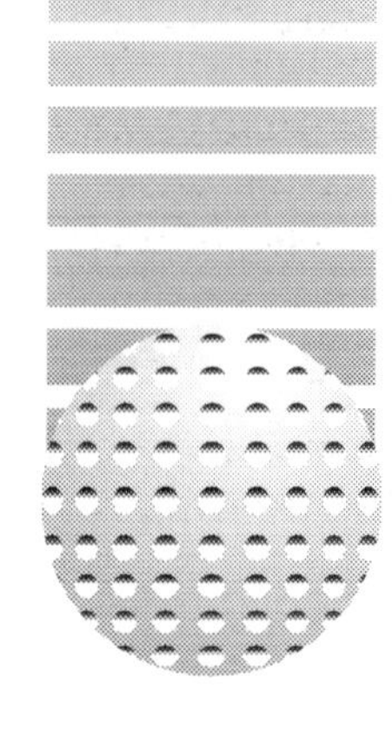

Bamburgh Castle Golf Club

NO golfing trip to the Northumberland coast would be complete without sampling the delights of Bamburgh.

The views from the clifftop course are sensational and when the gorse is in full flower the course is an absolute picture.

But club officials can get a little tetchy about glossy magazines which carry articles with photographs of the castle and the Farne Islands without showing the true nature of the course.

They do have a point. Although it measures only 5,465 yards, with a par of 68, the course is great fun to play, blending plenty of birdie opportunities with an almost ever-present potential for disaster.

Not that there will be many birdies on the first three holes.

A rare feature of the course is that it begins with two par threes, but at 182 and 213 yards both need solid strikes, while a glance ahead and to the right off the first tee reveals a steep drop to the beach.

The third is the first of several blind holes. But with the green 510 yards distant, you don't need to worry about the pin position until you have safely negotiated the marker post on the brow of the hill.

The fourth, known as Cheviot View, is the only other par five on the course.

There are four more par threes to come, however, starting with the sixth, which has the rare distinction for a supposed one-shotter of being the stroke one hole, mainly because it is 224 yards uphill.

The other par threes are all decidedly tricky. None more so than the eighth, a lovely little hole which is played from an elevated tee across a small valley to a saddle-shaped green surrounded by gorse and rocky outcrops.

The 14th is a similar hole coming back the other way, and after pausing to take in the panorama from the best vantage point on the course you will hopefully be suitably inspired to tackle the excellent 404-yard 15th.

A well-struck downhill drive should give you the opportunity to carry the valley in front of the green with a medium iron.

The 16th is a superb driving hole, back across the valley and through another one, which will assist a slight draw and carry a well-struck shot to the green.

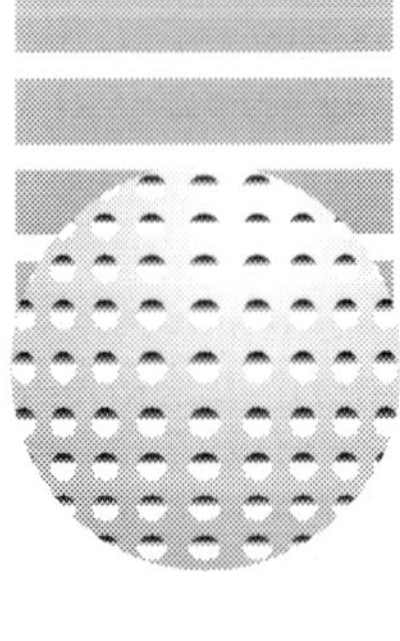

Bamburgh's tricky 8th hole

At 268, 260 and 314 yards, the last three holes all offer birdie chances. But while the 16th has its own perils, the last two both have out of bounds dangerously close on the right.

The 17th again offers magnificent views, down to the clubhouse with the sea and the Farne Islands beyond, and the castle away to the right.

If the 18th is a slightly disappointing finish, that's only because of the splendour of what has gone before.

The sturdy clubhouse gives the impression of having been built to withstand the sternest of buffetings from the weather.

Built in 1904, when the club moved from its original links site south of the castle, it provides a very cosy,

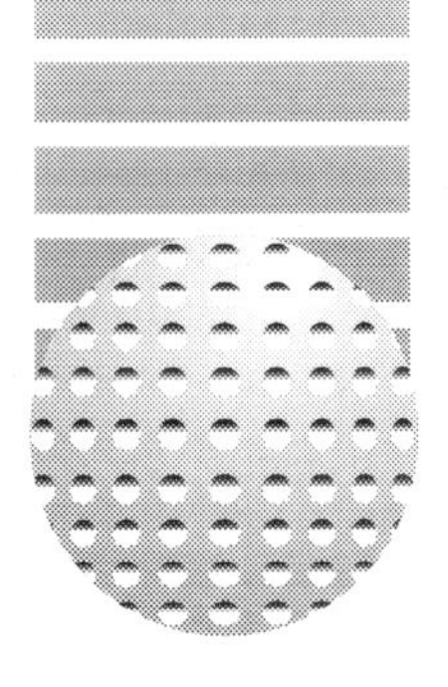

welcoming and unpretentious retreat.

It stands alongside a car park where the recent application of Tarmac did not meet with the universal approval of the members – perhaps because it is too big a concession to the modern age.

They certainly can't complain about misuse of their money as the 1994 membership fee was a mere £100, including the VAT.

The green fee is £23, but the course is closed to visiting societies at the height of the summer as many of the 650 members are holiday-makers who come for two weeks a year and expect unlimited access.

If you are thinking of joining their ranks, the bad news is that a waiting list was brought into operation in 1993.

For a wonderful course, though, that makes golfing holidays in this part of the world a real treat, then Bamburgh really does have to be high on the list for those who enjoy a testing time around a wonderfully scenic course.

There is enough of a challenge to make for a stern test – so don't be too distracted by those quite magnificent views.

FACTFILE

Address: Bamburgh Castle Golf Club, The Wynding, Bamburgh Northumberland NE69 7DE

Telephone: (01668) 314378

How to get there: Turn off A1 between Alnwick and Berwick on B1341 or B1342 for Bamburgh Village. turn left opposite Lord Crew Arms and into The Wynding

Course length: 5,465

Par: 68

Green fees: April-Oct £23 per round and £35 per day weekdays, £30 per round weekends and bank holidays

Special packages: Out of season deals available on request

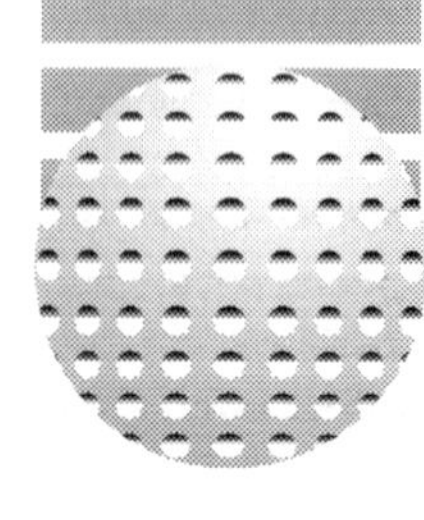

Newbiggin

Address: Clubhouse, Newbiggin-by-the-Sea, Northumberland, NE64 6DW

Telephone: (01670) 817344

How to get there: Village off the A197, 16 miles north of Newcastle and eight miles east of Morpeth. The club is at the eastern end of the village, next to Church Point Caravan Park.

Course: Links course, 18 holes, 6,423 yards

SSS: 71.

Founded: July 1884

Visitors: Welcome after 10am, but not on competition days.

Green fees: Available on application.

Special packages: Apply to the club secretary

Further information: Bar meals, lunch, dinner except Tuesdays. Snooker.

Ryton

Address: Ryton Golf Course, nr Clara Vale, Ryton, Tyne and Wear

Telephone: (0191) 4133737

How to get there: Situated on the Newcastle to Hexham on the south side of the river. Go through Blaydon, Ryton and take the road signposted Clara Vale.

Course length: 6,250 yards, 18 holes

SSS: 69

Special features: Second hole is particularly challenging. There are out of bounds on both sides and the shape of the hole makes it difficult. Has only been an 18-hole golf course for 12 years, nine-hole previously.

Founded: 1881

Visitors: Every weekday. Weekends – parties only.

Green fees: Weekday £8 with member, £12 non, £18 per day, weekends parties only £16.

Special packages: Parties on weekends at £16 each.

Hotels: Copthorne Hotel, Newcastle.

Further information: New clubhouse due to open

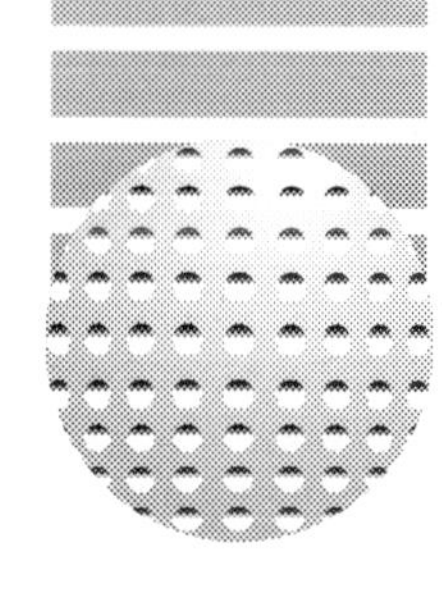

Seahouses Golf Club

GOLF at Seahouses provides a breath of fresh air in more ways than one. While the town centre seems out of step in this part of the world by dancing to the tune of fish restaurants and amusement arcades, the golf club remains a warmly welcoming haven of peace.

At only 5,150 yards off the yellow tees, it is a gentle stroll round this seaside course. But when you stand trembling on the tenth tee you are well aware that it's no doddle.

While the superb par three tenth will live longest in the memory, the relaxing atmosphere, fanned by the sea breezes, will also send you away with a warm glow.

The fact that it's a tight course, crammed into 70 acres, means there is not a lot of margin for error.

Since the only par five was created by lengthening the second in 1992, the par of 67 has been beaten only once – by local newsagent Keith Johnston, who shot a 64 on Captain's Day in 1993.

The course is considered good enough to stage county events and among the golfers it has produced are former European Tour player Gary Logan and the 1986 England Schoolboys champion Mark Dawson.

Straddling the main road on the southern approach to the town, the course does not at first sight present a particularly attractive challenge.

Holes three to eight, on the inland side of the road, are laid out on reclaimed marshland and are the most visible.

Apart from the ditches which can catch the unwary, this is fairly featureless terrain, although the 327-yard eighth, with the road running along its left-hand flank, is a good hole with a tight approach to an elevated green.

Back across the road, the ninth shares its fairway with the 18th and it's as well to remember that you are aiming for the red flag.

Then comes the unforgettable tenth. Known as Logan's Loch – named after former E.G.U. president George, the club's most famous son – it's 159 yards off the back tee across what at first sight looks like a long sea inlet, but is, in fact, freshwater.

If the wind is coming off the sea, this hole requires a solid and precise strike off the elevated tee to hit the narrow green. It's only 123 yards off the front tee, but if there's any

The view from behind Seashouses 10th green

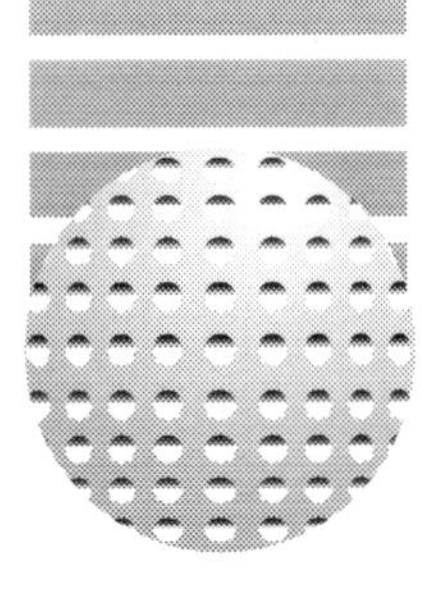

breeze at all it's all too easy to fall fatally short.

The next three holes are good par fours running back and forth from the clifftop, with the 13th green providing fine views of the town and the Farne Islands.

Then come two contrasting par threes along the cliff edge.

The 14th measures 211 yards off the back, while the 15th is the most daunting 116 yards imaginable across a deep cove. If you miss the green it had better be on the right.

There are three good par fours to finish, all with trouble on the left – first it's water, then the beach, then the road. Hookers will not be happy here.

The club was founded as a nine-holer in 1913 and extended to 18 holes in the early Seventies, partly under the guidance of one of the club's most prominent members, George Logan, a former president of the English Golf Union.

The work was carried out mainly by members and secretary John Stevens talks of the eighth green being laid in snow and the 16th in pouring rain: 'the turf was floating,' he says.

FACTFILE

Address: Seahouses Golf Club, Beadnell Road, Seahouses, Northumberland NE68 7XT

Telephone: (01665) 720794

How to get there: Off A1 five miles north of Alnwick on the B1340

Course length: 5,387

SSS: 66

Founded: 1913

Visitors: Welcome

Green fees: £15 weekdays, £20weekends

The original clubhouse was a First World War army billet and the current one was built in 1976 and refurbished to a very comfortable standard in 1992.

There is no professional, but regular coaching is arranged through the summer for the 74 junior members, with the Golf Foundation meeting half of the cost.

The club decided to take in 25 new members in 1994, and at the time of our visit there were still eight vacancies. At £125 a year, membership is well worth snapping up.

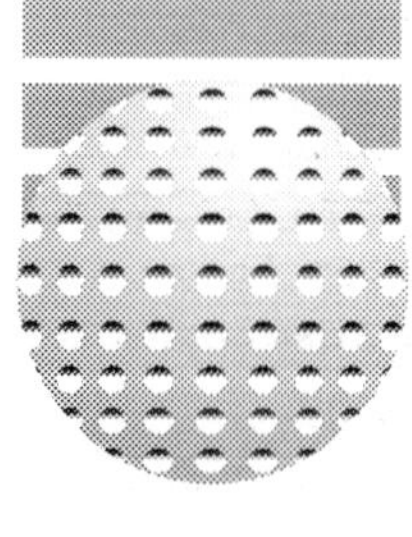

Arcot Hall

Address: Dudley, Cramlington, Northumberland NE23 7QP
Telephone: (0191) 236 2794
How to get there: One mile east of A1 off A1068 near the Holiday Inn
Course: 18 holes, 6,6389 yards, parkland
SSS: 70
Founded: 1910
Visitors: Welcome weekdays and non-competition weekends
Green fees: On application
Special packages: Societies not weekends. Lunches and teas.

Allendale

Address: Thornley Gate, Allendale, Hexham
Telephone: (0191) 267 5875
How to get there: Ten miles south west of Hexham on the Nenthead road B6305
Course: 9 holes, 4,488 yards
SSS: 63
Founded: 1907
Special features: Meadowland course
Visitors: No visitors August Bank Holiday Monday otherwise no restrictions but competitions have preference
Green fees: On application
Special packages: Societies by arrangement
Further information: Kettle and cooker provided, charge for electricity

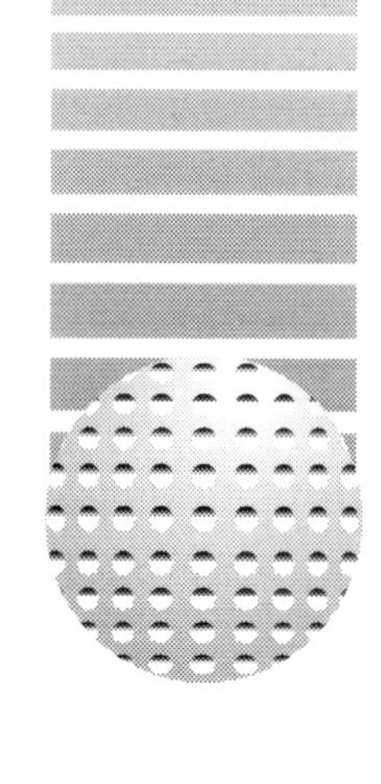

Northumberland golf club

No reference to golf courses in the North of England would be complete without featuring the Northumberland club inter-twined with the Racecourse at Gosforth Park.

The mere mention of the architects responsible for the championship layout should give an indication of its stature, Harry Shapland Colt and latterly James Braid being commissioned to design the course after the club moved from its original site on the Town Moor in 1898.

The very first club house was near the start of the straight mile beyond the present 13th green, a situation convenient to the Killingworth railway station from which golfers walked or rode in style in a pony and trap.

However, early in the 20th century the tram system was extended to the western entrance of the park and by 1913 the club had built and moved into the present club house.

The current course contains many of the original features with the Racecourse continuing to affect play on at least eight holes and the layout is a good test of golf needing length and accuracy, especially in a westerly wind which makes for a very tough finishing stretch.

The first is an inviting downhill tee shot and short pitch to the green which is angled well right, but the second is extremely tough, a 432-yard par 4 with a stream and out-of-bounds down the right.

Back to back par 5s give an opportunity to clinch a shot back from the card before a tough 186-yard par 3 brings one back to earth.

The 13th may prove unlucky for some at 481 yards, a par 4 with trees on the right and Racecourse to the left added to a tightly situated green.

The par 5 15th begins the punishing final run-in invariably against the prevailing wind, the 16th requiring a long carry over the Racecourse with the knowledge that anything less than perfect will be harshly punished and no matter how well the drive is struck the second shot still requires at best a long iron.

The 17th is also a tricky hole and the course concludes with a scenic hole with the green under the shadow of the club house.

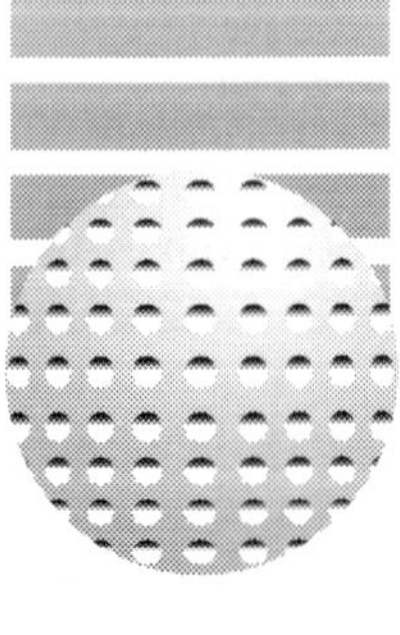

The drive is again over the Racecourse rails and the second invariably a medium iron played uphill over the sweeping fairway and bunkers to the large green.

The club has played host to a number of national championship events, both amateur and professional, the most notable being the English Amateur in 1972 when local lad Harry Ashby, a member at nearby Consett, won the first of his two titles beating Roger Revell 5 and 4 in the well attended final.

The Northumberland is seeped in tradition and is in many ways exclusive, however, with a letter of introduction and prior arrangements it is well worth a visit.

FACTFILE

Telephone: (0191)-236-2009

Address: High Gosforth Park, Newcastle upon Tyne NE3 5HT

Location: Situated off A6125 four miles north of Newcastle city centre

Course: Undulating parkland course, 18 holes, 6640 yards, SSS 72, designed by H.S. Colt and James Braid, founded 1898.

Visitors: Weekday by reservation with secretary and letter of introduction

Green fee: £30 weekdays, £35 weekends (bookings only)

Hotels: Gosforth Park and Holiday Inn.

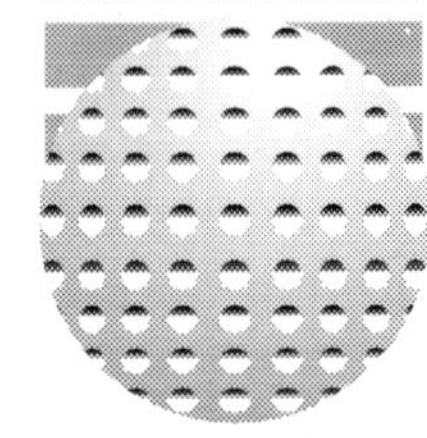

Matfen Hall Golf Club

A Jewel in the Northumberland countryside

Set in the Estate of the impressive and imposing Matfen Hall, we offer a lovely 6,744 yard Par 72 Parkland Course with rolling fairways, mature trees and natural water hazards.

Visitors are very welcome with no restrictions

Wide range of accommodation available locally

Call Dawn or John Harrison (Director of Golf) on

(01861) 886500

or write:

Matfen Hall Golf Club, Maften, Newcastle-upon-Tyne, Northumberland

Location: 12 miles west of Newcastle, just north of the A69

GB16

Is your wife fed up with early tee-off times?

Let her stay in bed and have breakfast here instead -

Full English Breakfast
£4.50

After a late day on the course has your wife given your dinner to the dog?

Why not rest your clubs here at the Cott and have your evening meal with us -

3 Course Meal £9.00 per person

All meals by prior arrangement with our cook (Jan)

Special rates for parties of 8 and over

A perfect setting for overnight stay for golfers everywhere

Ideally situated on the A1, giving easy access to all major golf courses in North Northumberland.

Why not rest your swing, and hole up for the night and not worry about being over par (in the comfort stakes). Stay in our friendly family run guest house.

We offer you:

Bed/Breakfast & Evening Meal	**£24.50 per person**
Bed/Breakfast	**£15.50 per person**

The Cott and Etive Cottages are set in their own well appointed gardens, with unrestricted views over local countryside.
Situated on the A1 above the village of Warenford only 12 miles north of the market town of Alnwick and 4 miles to Bamburgh, Seahouses and the beautiful Northumbrian coast

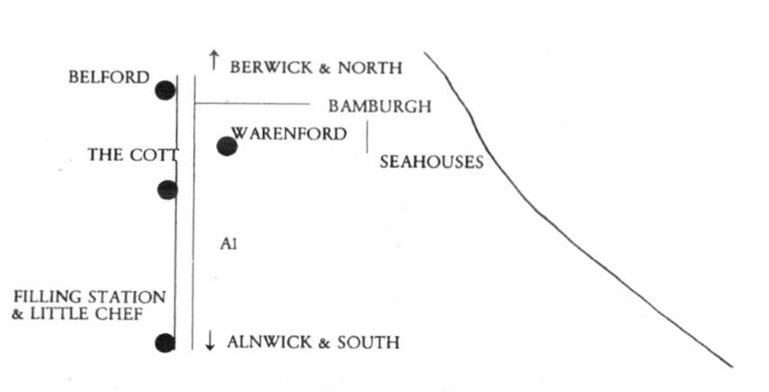

GB8

The 4th hole at Stressholme, Darlington

Putting at the Par 3 4th at Boldon

The Beamish Park Hotel

STAY AND PLAY

Incorporating the latest innovative technology, our super, bright, brand new Golf Driving Range now offers everyone the chance to improve their golf swing in the beautiful countryside surrounding the Beamish Park Hotel Our 4 Crown Highly Recommended Hotel and Award-winning Restaurant offers an excellent choice of good food and accommodation.

Rounds of Golf can be arranged at several of the beautiful courses within easy reach of the Beamish Park Hotel - Beamish, Whickham, Hobson and South Moor, or our own 20-bay floodlit driving range offers video playback facilities, PGA Expert Tuition for all levels (by appointment) and an excellent selection of Corporate and Group packages

Special "Golfing Break" accommodation rates are available for individuals, small groups and large parties

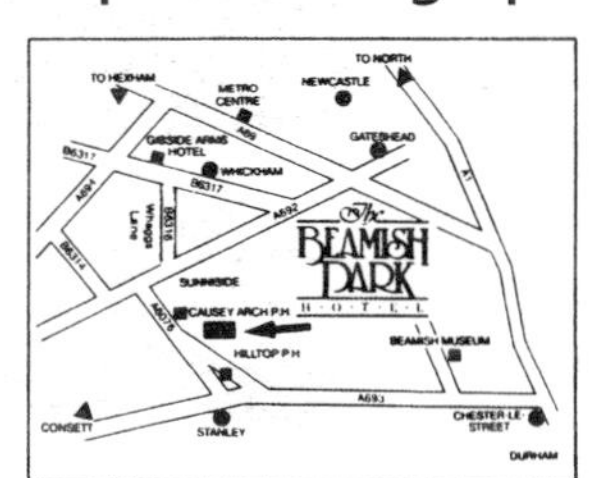

For Prices, or further details

The Beamish Park Hotel, Beamish Burn Road, Marley Hill, Newcastle upon Tyne NE16 5EG

Tel. (01207) 230666 Fax (01207) 281260

GB7

DURHAM

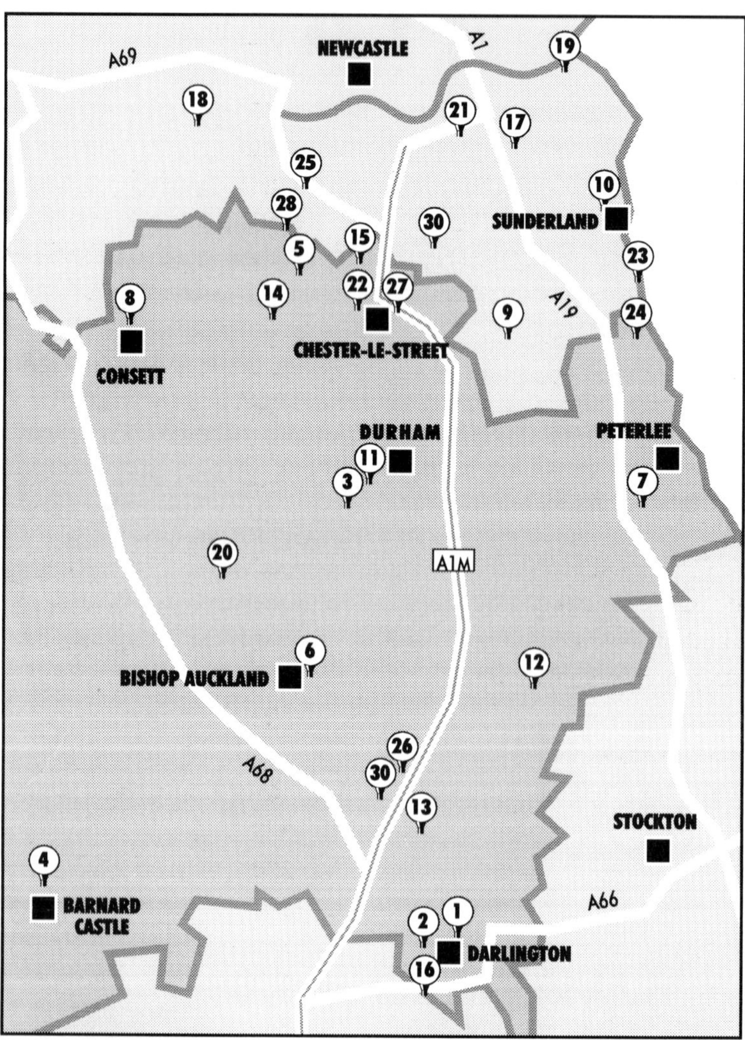

1 Darlington
2 Stressholme, Darlington
3 Brancepeth Castle
4 Barnard Castle
5 Beamish Park
6 Bishop Auckland
7 Castle Eden
8 Consett
9 Houghton-le-Spring
10 Wearside GC, Sunderland
11 Durham City
12 Knotty Hill, Sedgefield
13 Hall Garth, Coatham Mundeville
14 South Moor
15 Ravensworth
16 Blackwell Grange, Darlington
17 Boldon
18 Tyneside, Ryton
19 South Shields
20 Crook
21 Heworth
22 Roseberry Grange, Pelton
23 Ryhope
24 Seaham
25 Whickham
26 Woodham, Aycliffe
27 Chester-le Street
28 Hobson Municipal, Burnopfield
29 Moat House, Washington
30 Newton, Aycliffe

Durham courses

Darlington Golf Club

NOTHING but the best is good enough at Darlington Golf Club. The club which boasts the highest number of low handicap players in Durham, and includes Ian Botham among its members, needs a stage fit for them to parade their skills.

Darlington is considered one of the finest non-championship courses in the North-East.

Established in 1908 at Skerningham Woods, the club moved to its current site adjacent to Green Lane, Harrowgate Hill, in 1915. A picture to mark the occasion is displayed in the clubhouse.

But it was in 1957 when the club embarked upon an extensive tree-planting programme that the course took on its present character.

At 6,251 yards, the parkland course is by no means long. One of its most unusual features is that it has six par threes, each providing its own tricky test, while several other holes have hidden perils to test even the most accomplished golfer.

The construction of the greens by Augusta architect Dr Alastair MacKenzie also makes the course a haven for the putting connoisseur.

The third, 172 yards with a triple-tiered green guarded by five bunkers and with out of bounds to the left and back of the green, was described by top South African player Hugh Baiocchi as one of the best par threes he had ever played.

The seventh and ninth holes are also tricky par threes. The seventh is surrounded by bunkers and flanked by fir trees, while the ninth also has an abundance of bunkers and a burn guarding the front edge of the green. The 13th is an exacting test of golf, measuring 437 yards and with out of bounds all the way down the left.

Darlington's abundance of category one golfers have gained several county and union titles. Their finest hour came in 1989 when representing Durham in the English Clubs Team Championship at Southport and Ainsdale. Darlington led at the halfway stage by eight shots thanks to magnificent rounds of 68 by John Howson and Phil Steadman.

Unfortunately they had to settle for joint runners-up slot after being overhauled by Ealing who had England internationals Ricky Willison, Jerome O'Shae and Andy Rogers on their side.

The club's stature has also been enhanced by representatives of County and Union. Both Ken Rum-

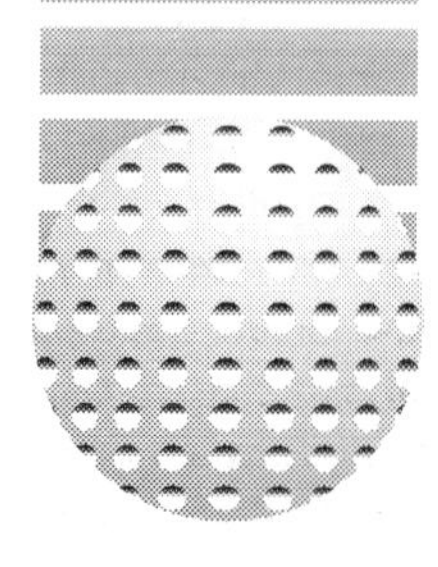

The 15th at Darlington Golf Club

ıey and Syd Liddle, the club's ınswer to Abbot and Costello, are ıast presidents of the Teesside Jnion, while the club's Durham County executive representative, Dennis Green, is chairman of the ounty coaching committee and also ıast president of the Durham County Veterans' Association.

Visitors wishing to complete their outing with a visit to the 19th will not be disappointed.

After building up an excellent reputation at the Coal Hole freehouse near Durham, Barry Millward and wife Kath went into early retirement. But much to the delight of club members they needed another chal-

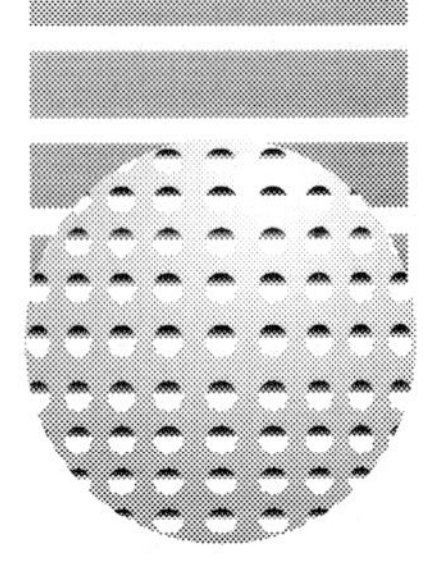

lenge and moved to Darlington Golf Club in 1988.

Barry offers a selection of draught and hand-pump beers and a choice of three lagers, described by the witty Dunelmian as 'standy up, lay down or go to sleep' depicting their various strengths.

A clubhouse extension coasting £100,000 in 1993 transformed the locker room, shower and lounge facilities.

Darlington is not an awesome test of golf and its terrain is far from physically demanding.

But it provides a fair test on a course which is invariably in excellent condition and has enough subtlety to bring the best out of the thinking golfer.

The club has a fine roll of honour including:

1957 Alf Owen,
Durham County matchplay champion
1976-77-78 Teeside Union A Divison champions
1979-80-81 and **'92** Teesside Union B Division champions
1977 Durham County Boys championship A K Green
1978 Teesside Union Boys champion A K Green
1980-81-82 and **'86** the NYSD Interclub team champions
1977-88 and **'90** A K Green Teesside Union matchplay champion
1984 A K Green Durham County matchplay champion
1989 J Howson Teesside Union matchplay champion
1982 and **'84** S Thompson Teesside Union boys champion
1982 and **'89** Durham Club champions
1988 Durham County mixed foursomes J Howson and Miss L Rochester
1989 English clubs team championship runners-up
1991 W Bell, Durham Junior Strokeplay champion
1990-93 J Howson, North Northumberland champion
1992 Mark Brooksbank, Teesside Union, matchplay champion
1992 J Howson and P Steadman Northumberland and Durham foursomes champions
1994 G Charlton NYSD Champion

FACTFILE

Address: Darlington Golf Club, Green Lane, Darlington, Co Durham

Telephone: (01325) 462955.

How to get there: North east of town on the A1150

Green Fees: weekdays £22 (£10 with member); weekends – members only.

Course length: 6,251 yards.

SSS: 70

Special packages: Rates on application to the club secretary on (01325) 463936.

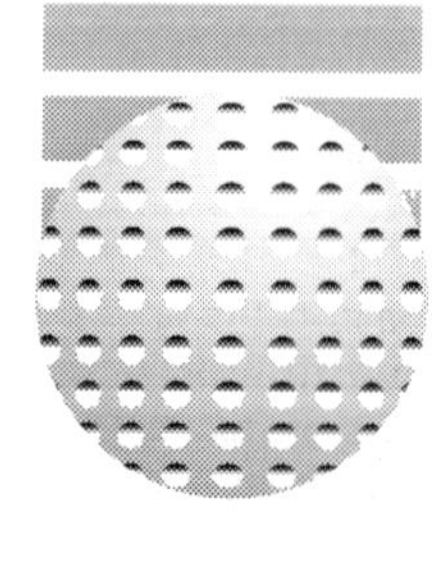

Stressholme Golf Centre

THE magical moments of Wembley 1973 are now a distant memory for former Sunderland striker Billy Hughes.

The man who helped Sunderland Football Club to a magical FA Cup win is now involved in a different kind of game altogether – and he is loving every minute of it.

After several years as steward at Stressholme, Darlington's municipal golf club, he is deeply involved in the club's remarkable transformation; almost a fairytale of its own.

Opened in 1976, it has always been acknowledged as a testing course, measuring 6,511 yards and providing a daunting finish, with the last five holes all over 400 yards.

But with queues of 70 not uncommon on the first tee and many of them novices with no regard for the etiquette of the game, it came to be regarded as a no-go area for many self-respecting golfers.

All that has changed since a division of Darlington Council named Contract Services won the tender to run the club under the Privatisation Act. The installation of a computer booking system plus course wardens and a starter on the first tee at peak times has revolutionised the club.

In 1992 it was re-named Stressholme Golf Centre with the emphasis on quality on and off the course.

The facilities were extended in 1994 with the opening of a £160,000 floodlit driving range.

It all adds up to much-improved business for Billy Hughes, who ran pubs in Derby, Sunderland and Gateshead after hanging up his boots, but is now perfectly settled at Stressholme.

'It helps that I love the game,' he said. 'I wish I'd had the chance to take it seriously earlier in life. When I'm not behind the bar I'm usually on the course or the practice ground.

'I get invited to a few pro-ams along with five or six of my old team-mates such as Bobby Kerr and Bob Moncur, not to mention Bob Stokoe.

'We have a good laugh, telling the same old stories about what happened 20-odd years ago. But golf is my passion now.'

A five-handicapper, he has won the club championship twice but is expecting more competition as better golfers are attracted to the club.

More importantly for him, business in the clubhouse has greatly increased.

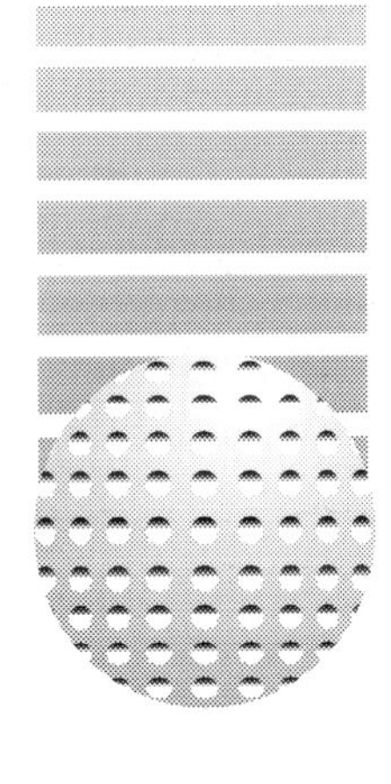

Stressholme Golf Centre

View from the Driving Range at Stressholme.Insets: Billy Hughes now and in 1973 during the glory days of Sunderland AFC

'The changes we have made have worked wonders,' he said. 'Players used to queue for hours on the first tee, but now they book their time and meet half an hour beforehand in the bar.'

Hughes is also involved in encouraging better standards of dress and etiquette. 'I hate the snobbishness you get at a lot of golf clubs, but I believe if you are going to play a sport you should be properly turned out for it. And etiquette is very important in golf. We used to get people playing in groups of six, sharing clubs and becoming abusive when they were asked to let people through. With a few polite reminders from the starter and the warders none of that happens anymore.'

Heavily involved in the centre's transformations was Tim Jenkins.

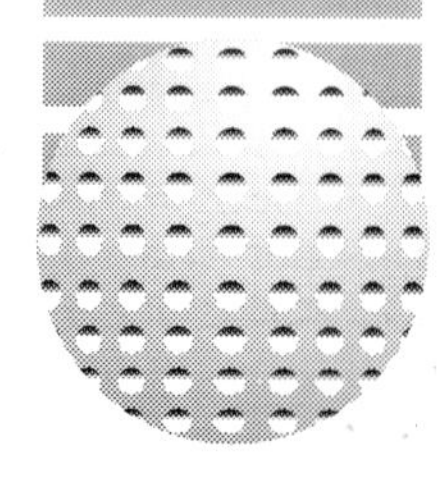

He was assistant professional at Darlington from 1976-84, became the full professional at Castle Eden and then took over at Stressholme in 1992 before moving to Mayfair driving range, Seaton Carew.

'I knew there was a lot of untapped potential at Stressholme,' he said.

'More than 20 pros applied for the job and at the interview we were asked to write down what we would do with the place.

'I wanted it to become a centre of golfing excellence.'

In most respects Jenkins succeeded – but the recession meant that his own shop business fell short of expectations and in 1994 he left, to be replaced by Robert Lister, formerly at Aycliffe.

The course may not be the most scenic in the world, at one point affording views of Darlington sewage works, but it is certainly challenging and very well-kept.

FACTFILE

Address: Stressholme Golf Club, Snipe Lane, Darlington Co. Durham.

Telephone: (01325) 363872

How to get there: Eight miles north of Scotch Corner. Take A167 turnoff from A1. Club signposted at roundabout opposite garage.

Green Fees: weekdays £8; weekends £9.50.

Course length: 6,511 yards

SSS: 71.

Special packages: Discounts available on new driving range if playing that day.

A new, state-of-the-art driving range, considered to be one of the most modern in the country, is located on the site of the former first hole. The original second remains. It is a difficult 452-yard par four featuring a downhill to a green nestling in a loop of the River Skerne.

The Skerne also comes into play on the next two holes, particularly at the 106-yard fourth, where the tee-shot has to carry a bend in the river.

Of the other three par threes, the ninth and 11th are both over 200 yards, with the latter being fiendishly hard to hit because of its narrow green well protected by bunkers. There is some respite at 12 and 13 before the demanding finish begins with the 504-yard 14th.

Many a good card is ruined on the closing stretch, but now that the queues and the six-balls have gone it's a challenge serious golfers will want to repeat.

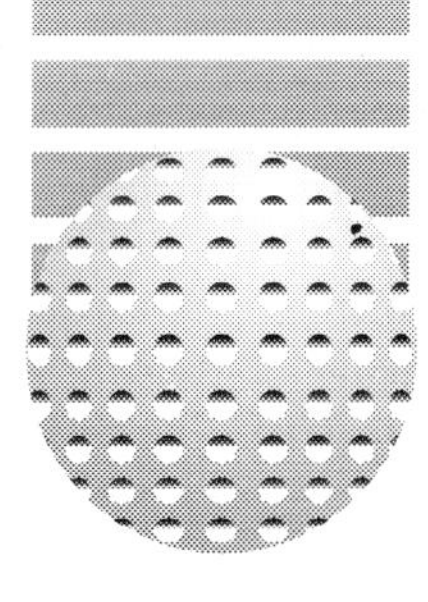

Barnard Castle Golf Club

Barnard Castle, always one of the most enjoyable courses in the North-East, underwent changes during 1993 and 1994 which added considerably to its challenge.

Situated on part of the old Raby Estate with uninterrupted views up Teesdale to Cross Fell and Mickle Fell, it derives much of its charm from the four natural becks which meander gently through the course, coming into play on 15 holes.

But before the re-design the course was considered very flattering to players of lower handicap at just over 5,800 yards. Indeed, the standard scratch was set at three shots below the course's par of 71.

This prompted the club to seek further land to lengthen the course, and after many years of negotiations with their landlords they acquired 40 acres to the left of the old seventh and ninth holes.

The new layout includes three new greens and the only holes where there will be no alterations are the first two and the much-loved 17th.

One of the course's weaknesses has been that it features six par threes, with three of them in the last four holes. Two of those, the old 15th and 16th have been combined to create a dog-leg par four. The overall effect is an increase in yardage to over 6,500, with a revised par from the championship tees of 73.

John Harrison, twice holder of the PGA North Region Club Professionals Championship, was associated with the club for 15 years, joining as assistant to his brother Phil in 1979. Phil was the club's first full professional as the pro had previously doubled up as head greenkeeper; the most famous in this dual role being Arthur Watson, who was instrumental in reconstructing the course after many holes were lost to the agricultural war effort. A monument to Arthur sits at the back of the ninth green.

Former Ryder Cup player Ken Bousfield was also a regular visitor when his father became station master at Barnard Castle. Ken Driver, who has recently retired as professional at Stocksfield, also gave unstinting commitment during his time at Barnard Castle.

Determined to continue the club's high profile of playing professionals, former England Boys and Durham County senior player Darren Pearce moved from Darlington to Barnard Castle as assistant and took over as full pro when Harrison moved to

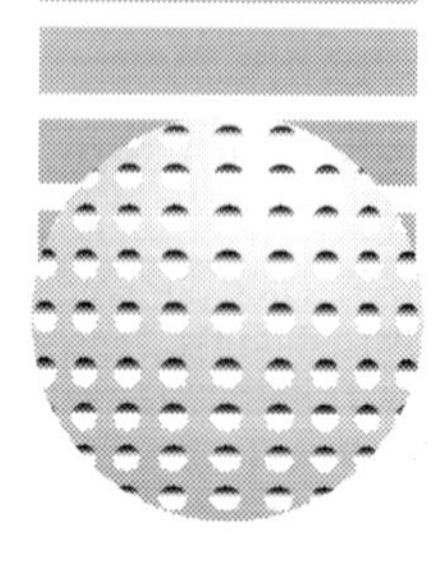

In reflective mood at the 4th hole, Barnard Castle

Matfen Hall in Northumberland when it opened in 1994

Golfers first played in the area in 1892, when the Teesdale Golf Club was formed. The Barnard Castle club was created on its current site six years later and a centenary committee has been formed to arrange events for 1998. The original clubhouse, which today serves as the greenkeeper's shed, was the pavilion at Darlington cricket ground.

The club had very much an artisan feel for many years, with members

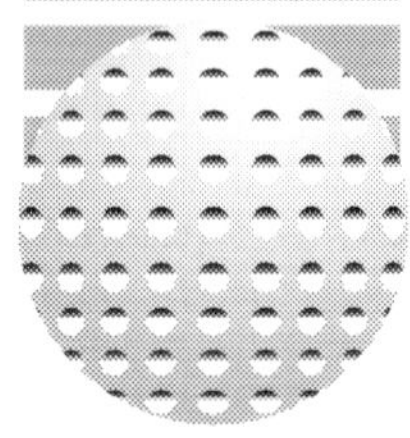

Barnard Castle Golf Club

helping out wherever possible, and in 1989 a tree-planting programme took place with Ron Caygill overseeing the operation.

Ron was known to many in the area as John Harrison's caddy and made a great contribution to the club. The six par threes produced plenty of the holes-in-one, with Sid Robinson, club treasurer for many years, leading the way with 13.

Members are awaiting the route of the town by-pass to be finalised as it could force them to build a new clubhouse near the site now occupied by the greenkeeper's shed.

While this would offer a superb view up Teesdale, it would mean the 18th hole would have to be scrapped. But under the new layout the tenth became a spare hole, which could be brought back into play.

FACTFILE

Address: Harmire Road, Barnard Castle DL12 8QN

Telephone: (01833) 38355

How to get there: On road from Barnard Castle to Egglestone, just past Glaxo factory

Course length: 5,838

SSS: 68

Special features: Becks to be crossed 15 times during round

Founded: 1898

Visitors: Welcome 9.45 am to noon and after 1.45pm

Green fees: £15 per day weekdays, £24 per day at weekends

The 17th would then become an excellent closing hole. A par four with the stream running down the fairway, it requires an accurate drive down the right followed by a pitch across the water to the green.

Only the extremely brave or very foolish attempt the narrow route down the left of the stream, especially with trees and out of bounds perilously close.

The first hole also oozes character. On the card it looks a gentle par four at 300 yards, but the stream runs down the left then cuts across immediately in front of the green, which lies hidden in a hollow.

The second is a par five into the prevailing wind, which comes down the valley. When it blows the 535-yard stroke index one hole can seem to go on forever and there are several more tough holes on the revised layout, which greatly enhances this beautiful corner of Durham.

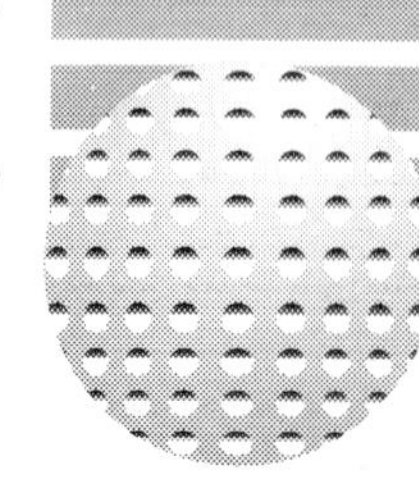

Crook

Address: Low Jobs Hills, Crook, Co Durham

Telephone: (01388) 762429

How to get there: Half-mile outside Crook on the A690 Durham to Willington road

Course length: 6,102 yards, 18 holes

Par: 70

Special features: There is a copse to contend with at the 12th. The 13th hole is one of the most difficult par 5 holes in Britain.

Founded: 1919

Visitors: Welcome at all times, parties must book at weekends.

Green fees: Weekday £8 members, £12 non-members, weekend £15 members, £20 without.

Special packages: During midweek for £19.50 party members can enjoy the course, plus coffee, biscuits, soup and sandwiches and three-course evening meal.

Hotels: Hotel in West Auckland is popular. Crook is a small place so most players stay in Auckland and Durham.

Further information: During the past two years the course has been altered considerably. The club is very friendly and the course is a tough test of players' ability.

Heworth

Address: Heworth Golf Course, Jingling Gate, Heworth, Gateshead.

Telephone: (0191) 469 2137

How to get there: On the Gateshead to Washington road on the edgte of Gateshead, situated along from the Black Bull on Leam Lane.

Course length: 6,459 yards, 18 holes

SSS: 71

Special features: Holds county competitions on a regular basis.

Founded: 1912

Visitors: Any weekday, weekends when there are no competitions..

Green fees: Weekday and weekends £14.

Special packages: For parties of 20 or more packages include 27 holes with a three-course meal, soup and sandwiches, biscuits and coffee.

Further information: Friendly reputation – visitors always want to return. The clubhouse includes an attractive lounge used for conferences.

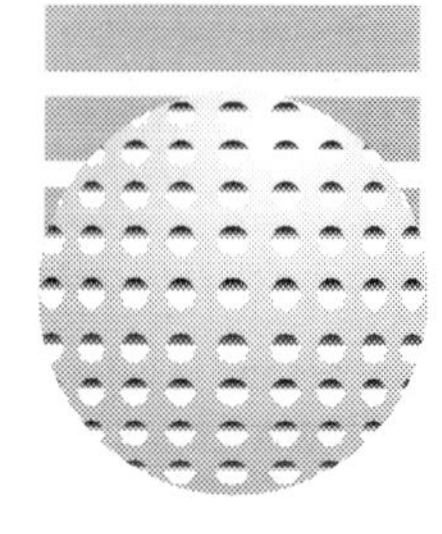

Brancepeth Castle Golf Club

BRANCEPETH Castle is widely acknowledged as the best inland course in Durham. Although the club regret that they did not have the finances to buy the imposing castle in the early 1980s, when it also attracted interest from Kojak star Telly Savalas, the members are delighted to play in what was once the estate's deer park.

Making full use of the deep, wooded ravine which comes into play on eight of the holes, the course is laid out in 140 acres of surprising beauty in an otherwise barren landscape south-west of Durham City.

Having negotiated the thickly wooded winding driveway which gives every impression of the tradesmen's entrance, the clubhouse, which occupies the original stables and coachhouse, emerges and visitors are immediately assured that this is no ordinary golf club.

The course was created in 1923 on the instructions of the then occupant of the castle Lord Boyne. It was designed by Harry S Colt, creator of such golfing masterpieces as Wentworth, St George's Hill and Pine Valley, USA.

The varied demands of the couse mean that counting ravines is the least of your worries, except if you happen to visit them all. The par threes are singled out as the key to scoring, and with three of the five being over 200 yards and the remaining two consisting of tee, green and scarcely little else from which to recover, this is hardly surprising.

The 155-yard second hole is played across the ravine from halfway down the bank. The green is cut into the far slope with the babbling brook below, and the only comfort is that the bank at the back of the green serves as a backstop.

There are no dull holes, but after the perils of the 585-yard sixth the highlight arrives at the ninth and tenth – Brancepeth's answer to Augusta's Amen Corner. If the bell of the adjacent St Brandon's church happens to toll, beware. It may well be for thee.

The 214-yard ninth, or garden hole, is played from yet another elevated tee over the ravine, to an appropriately coffin-shaped green which lies in the shadow of the castle. Accuracy is paramount as the right edge of the green falls away, leaving those who stray to this side a blind pitch second shot. The descent from the tee to green passes a magnificent fir tree planted by Queen Mary when

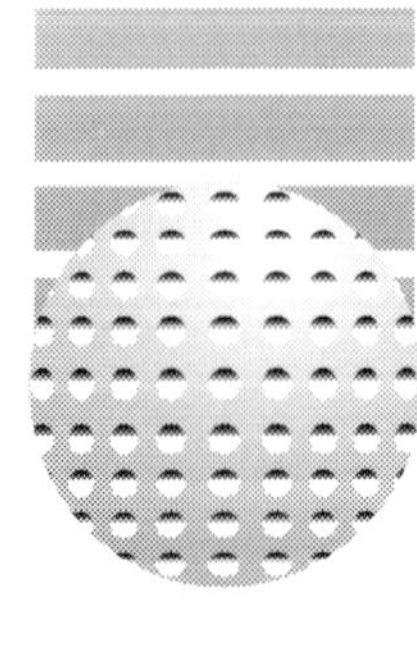

The 10th green at Brancepeth Castle Golf Club

View from the 7th green at Bishop Auckland Golf Club

The 9th hole at Brancepeth Castle

Princess of Wales. It acts as a natural umbrella to the rhododendrons on the banks of the stream, which is crossed via a wooden bridge.

The tenth, another long par three, is equally as difficult, going back across the ravine with the castle at your back. The 11th and 13th are par fours in excess of 430 yards, then come birdie chances at the 12th and 16th, both par fives, before the 18th provides a fitting resume of all that has gone before.

The hole demands a well-struck tee-shot over the ravine to a generous fairway, from which the uphill second shot will be blind for those who have only just cleared the trouble.

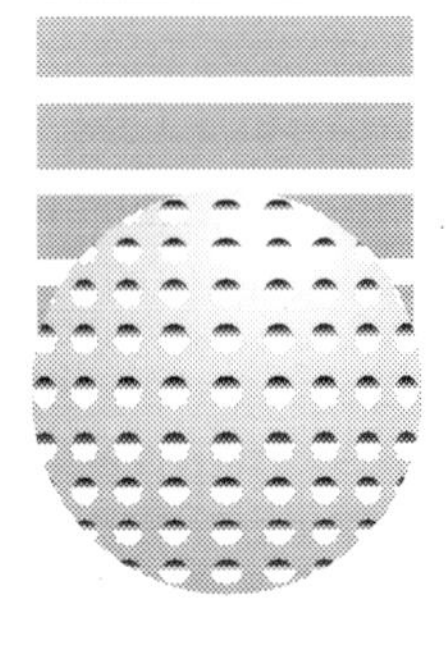

Brancepeth Castle Golf Club

Until around 15 years ago Brancepeth was a very exclusive club. But it became increasingly apparent that survival rested on a more universal approach and in the early Eighties the club took the unusual step of advertising for members and waiving the entrance fee.

This invitation was quickly taken up and the club now has a healthy membership in all categories in excess of 700. John Ross, a local lad who caddied at Brancepeth for pocket money in his teenage years, is one of the few salaried secretaries in the area. He took office in 1991, replacing Derek Carver who had served the club for many years and is an honorary member.

The club has had a number of distinguished members, most notably former Walker Cup player and Daily Telegraph golf correspondent Leonard Crawley, after whom the club's annual scratch open event is named. It was in this event in 1991 that Lancashire player Garry Boardman reportedly drank 15 pints of Guinness and ate two Vindaloo curries on the Friday night, then broke the course record with a 64 the following day.

FACTFILE

Address: Brancepeth Castle Golf Club, Brancepeth Village, Durham.

Telephone: (0191) 378 0075

How to get there: Four miles west of Durham City on A690 to Crook. Left at crossroads in village then slip road to left just before castle gates

Green Fees: Weekdays £24; weekends £30

Course length: 6,415

SSS: 71

Special deals: Reduced weekday rates for societies dependent on numbers.

J B Todd, five times winner of the Durham County Championship and former president of the EGU, is an honorary member of the club, which also boasts Harry Ashby, twice winner of the English Amateur Championship, as a former member.

Club professional David Howdon, a genial Georgie, adds his touch of colour to the club. He has taught in Germany and Sweden and has played on the African tour.

Brancepeth comes highly recommended as a club which combines the old and the new in perfect harmony. A visit can only be described as an uplifting experience.

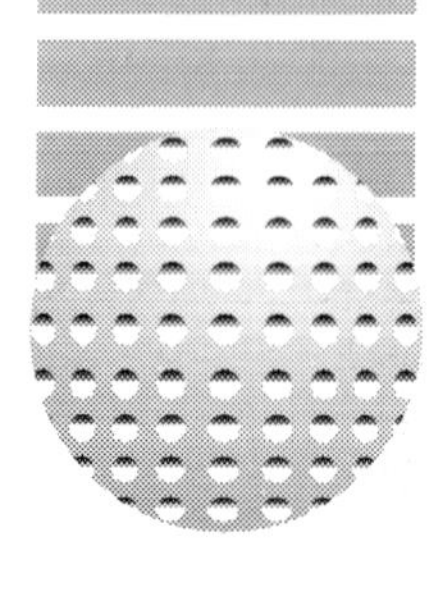

Whickham

Address: Whickham Golf Course, Hollinside Park, Whickham, Newcastle upon Tyne.

How to get there: Six miles west of Newcastle, one mile west of Whickham village.

Course length: 5,700 yards, 18 holes **SSS:** 69

Special features: First – most interesting and difficult first hole in the county. Good views of Derwent Valley.

Founded: 1911

Visitors: Monday to Friday, arrange through secretaries for parties.

Green fees: Weekday £20 per day, £8 member. Weekends £25.

Special packages: Negotiations for reduced fees, catering available.

Hotels: Beamish Park Hotel, Beamish. Gibside Hotel, Whickham. The Townley Arms.

Further information: Just bought 30 acres of land hoping to extend the course to championship length. Visitors very welcome. Course is scenic and beautiful, it's also situated two minutes from the MetroCentre.

Chester-le-Street Golf Course

Address: Lumley Park, Chester-le-Street, Co Durham.

How to get there: Half-a-mile east of Chester-le-Street near Lumley Castle.

Course length: 6,452 yards (from 1995) 18 holes

SSS: 69

Special features: Testing 5th par 4 at 458 yards. Good greens.

Founded:1909.

Visitors: Weekdays 9.30-12 and 1.30-3.30pm. Weekends very limited, no parties.

Green fees: weekday £20; weekend £25.

Special packages: Yes

Hotel: Lumley Castle Hotel, Lambton Arms Hotel.

Further information: All visitors must be members of a golf club with an official handicap.

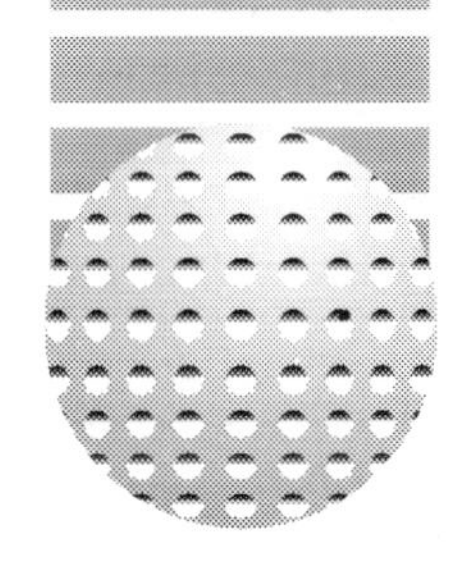

Houghton-le-Spring Golf Club

ONE of the most improved golf clubs in Durham over the last ten years, Houghton-le-Spring provides visiting parties with the best value for money in the area.

Coffee on arrival, lunch and a three course evening meal, together with 12 holes in the morning and 18 in the afternoon, is the weekday package offered to groups of eight or more at the amazing price of around £20.

Situated to the east of the town at Copt Hill, on the road to Seaham, the club has survived the ravages of economic decline in an area which has seen its once vibrant coal industry decimated.

The club, which has many ex-miners within its membership, has until recently led a hand to mouth existence since its inception in 1908, with minutes from their early meetings frequently reporting shortfalls of income versus expenditure.

The Durham County Advertiser chronicled the opening of the course on its current site in 1912 by Norman Robinson, the club's landlord and first chairman.

At the 1913 annual meeting, held at the Station Hotel in Fencehouses, the total membership of the club was reported as 74. A clubhouse was built in the 1920s at a cost of £233 and by 1935 the club had amassed 200 members.

It was around this time that the captain, R R Dodd, won the Durham County Championship two years running, while the chairman was former Sunderland Football Club supremo Sid Collins.

In the late 1970s the club leased more than 100 acres from the National Coal Board to enable them to extend the course to 18 holes. The rest of the land is owned partly by the club and partly by Lord Lambton.

The opening two holes are modest par fours with out of bounds on the right, while the well-bunkered par three third leaves little room for error from the tee.

The seventh is afforded the stroke index one at 433 yards played into the prevailing wind. A hedgerow either side of the fairway at driving length claims more than its fair share of casualties. The first half is rounded off with two superb holes.

The eighth, a downhill 225-yard par three, is flanked by the boundary fence all the way down the right and a par here is considered a bonus by most. The next two, both par fives along the wooded valley bottom, are

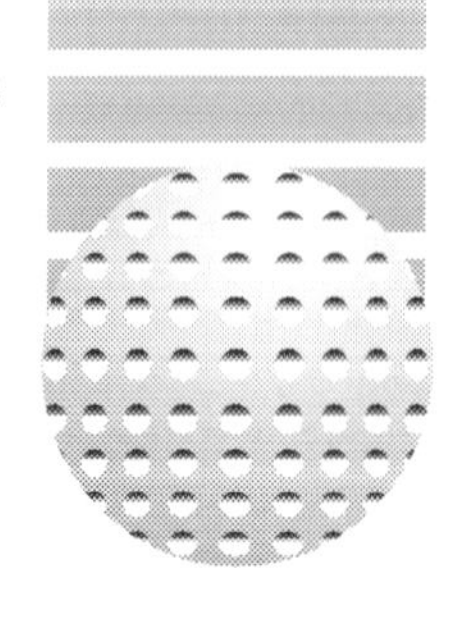

Houghton-le-Spring Golf Club

Houghton-le-Spring course

the signature holes at Houghton, played alongside Rough Dene Burn to the right.

The ninth also has two streams crossing its fairway, the first just beyond driving and the second some 30 yards short of the green. Nor does the tenth rely solely on length for its protection, as the dene continues to give the slicer nightmares.

The option of reaching in two by the graphite-wielding brutes must again be weighed against the threat of a large ditch guarding the front and right of a green which can only be described as unique.

The left half contains a number of shells and swales, while the right half is a classic basin. This puts even more emphasis on the approach shot as anything above or left of the cup requires the touch of a surgeon to escape the dreaded three putts.

The 11th is a driveable four, while the 15th is a sweeping downhill par five with internal out of bounds on the left. The last three holes will remind you that nothing is over until

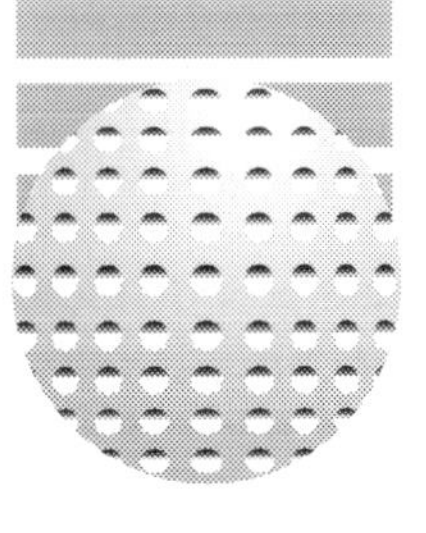

the fat lady exercises her vocal chords as they require the utmost concentration to avoid destroying your card.

The 16th has recently been remodelled and provides a canny test at 384 yards, while the uphill 17th plays well over its 348 yards with out of bounds on the right.

The finishing hole is another toughie at 426 yards, the key being a well struck tee shot. Out of bounds awaits on the right, while the clubhouse and surrounds make the approach to the green equally daunting.

Phil Newton, greenkeeper for 15 years, and his staff have worked hard with the inherent problems of the NCB land to provide very adequate greens throughout the year.

Recent success stories include John Hogg Jnr, winner of the 1980 North Durham League championship, who has played for Durham County on a number of occasions, while John Ellison is an excellent prospect. Ellison's finest hour came in the club's inaugural Houghton Feast Am-Am, when he shattered the course record with an amazing nine under par 63 on a foggy, miserable day which prompted one of his playing partners to comment that it is was one of the best rounds of golf he'd never seen.

Social activities are well supported in the clubhouse, which has been dubbed Colditz because it is so difficult to leave once you are there.

FACTFILE

Address: Houghton-le-Spring Golf Club, Copt Hill, Houghton-le-Spring, Tyne and Wear.

Telephone: (0191) 584 1198

How to get there: Half a mile from houghton-le-Spring on the A1085 Seaham Harbour road

Green Fees: Weekdays £18; weekends £22

Course length: 6,400

SSS: 71

Special deals: Parties playing 9 holes in morning and then 18 in the afternoon qualify for discounted meals in the recently refurbished clubhouse.

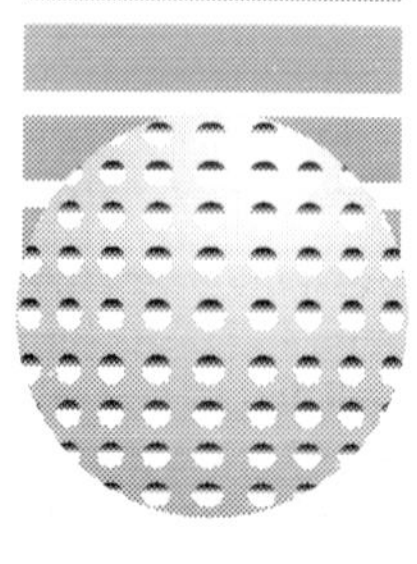

Bishop Auckland Golf Club

FEW clubs are as passionate and proud of their golfing history as Bishop Auckland, which was founded in 1894.

Situated at High Plains, the clubhouse, built in 1969, affords panoramic views across the Wear valley and the Bishops Palace, home of the Bishop of Durham, can be glimpsed among the trees.

Members claim it has the best views of any course in the county. It is certainly one of the most challenging.

The original nine holes were designed by Seaton Carew professional Jimmy Kaye for use by the student priests of the adjacent palace.

Kaye was again called upon 20 years later to extend the course to 18 holes.

Many notable developments within the club have been unearthed by long standing member Dick Longstaff, father of a former Durham County Youth champion John Longstaff, in researching a book for the club's centenary.

He found a ticket, priced at half a crown, (12.5p!) for an exhibition match staged at the club in 1906 between two of the forefathers of the modern game, J H Taylor and James Braid, who were reportedly paid eight guineas.

The land is still leased from the Church Commissioners and the bishop acts as the club's president.

The club appointed two prominent past captains to do the job again in the centenary year. Len Oughton, captain in 1976, has since served as president of both the Durham County Golf Union and Teesside Union, while Flo Clement was ladies' captain in 1961 and a former Durham County Ladies' president.

The club has achieved a long list of honours dating back to 1913 when H W Cummins won the Durham County Strokeplay championship.

In the last 20 years they have produced an unprecedented crop of young players, including Len Oughton's son David.

An England boy international, David won the county strokeplay title in 1976 as well as the matchplay equivalent on two occasions while clocking up more than 50 appearances for his county.

Lester Aisbitt, with whom Oughton won the Durham and Northumberland foursomes, has also contributed to five victories in the Clark Cup, the Durham County five-man team event and has partnered three-

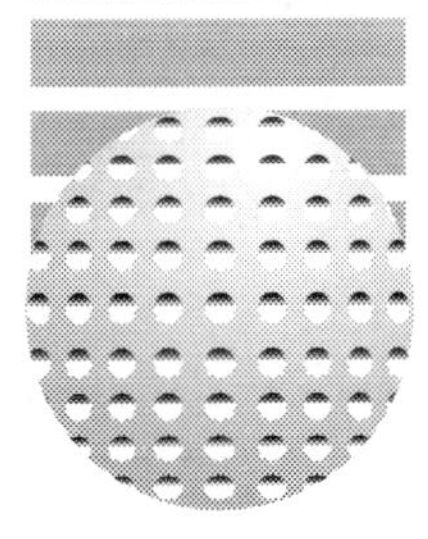

Bishop Auckland Golf Club

Teeing off from the seventh hole

times Durham Ladies champion Barbara Mansfield to a hat-trick of county mixed foursomes titles.

Lester's son Richard is one of a select band of players in the country playing off a plus handicap.

The course at first glance seems rather unbalanced in that there are only two par fours in the first 12 holes, while the last six holes are all par fours. The first hole affords little hint of what lies immediately ahead.

At under 300 yards it should catch out only the rustiest of swings, providing a modest stepping stone to the awaiting trio of 500-yard plus par fives.

The second and fourth are both played downhill to a green guarded by a small ravine.

The third, stroke index one, is an uphill slog with a spinney awaiting a slice off the tee and fairway bunkers mercilessly gathering errant second shots.

The fifth is a demanding 214-yard par three, while the ravine is at its most punishing on the 341-yard sixth before successive par threes provide a menacing challenge.

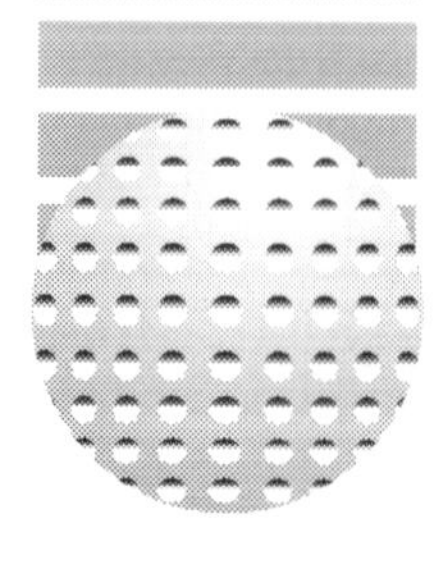

The 143-yard seventh is a lovely hole played along the widened valley of the ravine from an elevated tee to a green protected by a stream, trees and bushes. Although the temptation is to take advantage of the natural slope from the right, there is little margin for error.

The eighth sees the last of the stream, but it bows out in style as the 182-yard hole requires a carry of 160 yards to reach safety.

The first half is concluded with yet another par five, affectionately known as Thrombosis Hill.

The tenth and 12th are long par threes, while the 493-yard 11th supplies a welcome respite as long as fairway and greenside bunkers are avoided.

Just as you were thinking the par four was a thing of the past (having played six holes without one), the 13th presents a fitting retort at 438 yards.

The stroke index two hole hugs the out of bounds fence to the right, while a mature tree awaits the cautious drive up the left.

The 15th is another extremely tough par four and the 17th is another uphill test with the added irritation of an elevated green throwing all but the perfectly flighted shots off target.

The last, a 280-yard uphill par four, provides a perfect opportunity for a finishing birdie, provided the sand is avoided.

The club has an overall sporting feel with a high proportion of the members being ex-footballers or cricketers, including Glyn Thatcher, the enthusiastic club-secretary. Bishop Auckland is a glowing example of success breeding success, blending proud tradition with inevitable change and striking the perfect balance between competitiveness on the course and friendliness in the clubhouse.

FACTFILE

Address: Bishop Auckland Golf Club, High Plains, Bishop Auckland, Co Durham

Telephone: (01388) 602198

Green Fees: £20 round, £24 day weekdays weekends £26 round

Course length: 6,6420.

SSS: 71

Special deals: Groups of over 20 pay round rate for the day's golf.

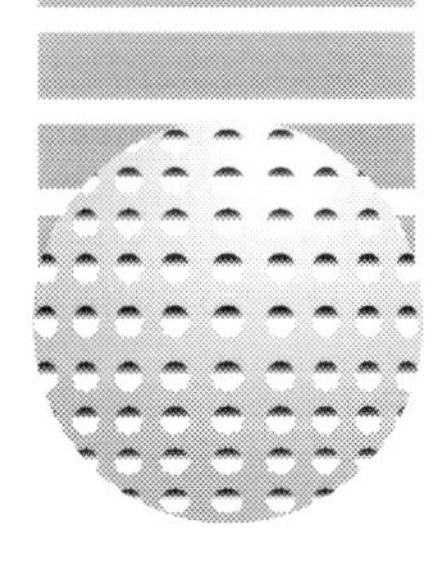

Castle Eden Golf Club

Standing on the first tee of the Castle Eden course it is difficult to ignore the proximity of the imposing Whitbread Brewery.

Indeed, for those who play the Royal and Ancient game for the purpose of reaching the 19th hole intact, only the magnificent views revealed opposite the Coopers refuge prevent an exodus to the bar.

The original owner of the brewery, J W Nimmo, formed the club after the first World War to provide recreation for his staff.

The clubhouse of the Dene Golf Club, a large army hut, was transported lock, stock and barrel from Ripon Barracks. The club was opened to the public in 1927 when it changed its name to the Castle Eden Golf Club.

It remained a nine-holer until 1968, when Whitbread sold the existing land for £25,000 and Peterlee Development Council made land available to extend the lay-out to 18 holes.

Sir Henry Cotton was commissioned to design the new nine holes and the layout is considered by many to provide one of the finest tests of golfing ability in the area.

Cotton's most controversial addition was the monstrous 620-yard 14th hole, uphill to a two-tiered green, with the original Nimmo family home giving a magnificent backdrop.

The members persevered with the hole for many years in deference to the architect but sanity prevailed in recent years, the hole being reduced to a more acceptable length.

The course has one of the most difficult starts in County Durham, the opening three holes all being in excess of 400 yards.

A respite is offered on the fourth and fifth, while the sixth, first of the par threes, is a daunting prospect for the higher handicapper, its 175 yards requiring a carry of 100 yards to avoid an all-too-inviting ravine.

The second par three, just under 200 yards, rounds off the first nine. The tenth is a reachable par five for the big hitters, while the 11th, another short hole, requires accurate club selection as there is precious little between the elevated tee and postage stamp green.

Another interesting example of historical architecture is visible from the 12th tee; that of the castle, former home of Colonel Burden, a local mine owner in the early part of the century. The building had fallen into disrepair after it was vacated by

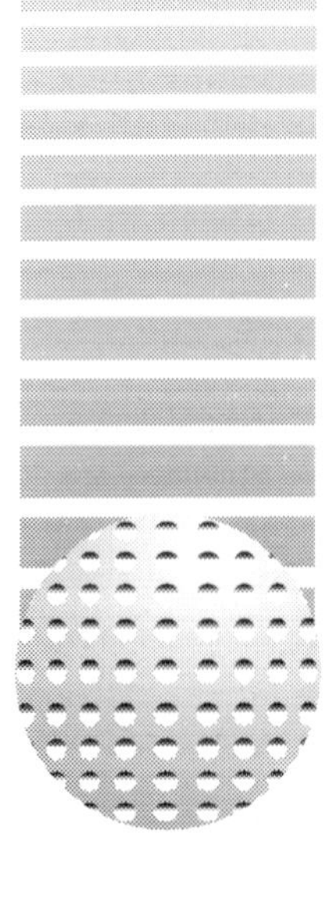

Teeing off at the 17th at Castle Eden

its original owner following his bankcruptcy but is being restored gradually, despite excessive costs. The 13th deserves its stroke index one billing, calling for a blind teeshot to a fairway which slopes away with a mature spinney awaiting errant shots to the right. The second shot is equally demanding to a green which slopes from back to front and left to right. Another interesting feature of this hole is a hollow to the left of the fairway, which is the site of an air crash during a training flight in the Second World War. Club captains, accompanied by the local vicar, still visit the spot on Remembrance Day, marking the site with a

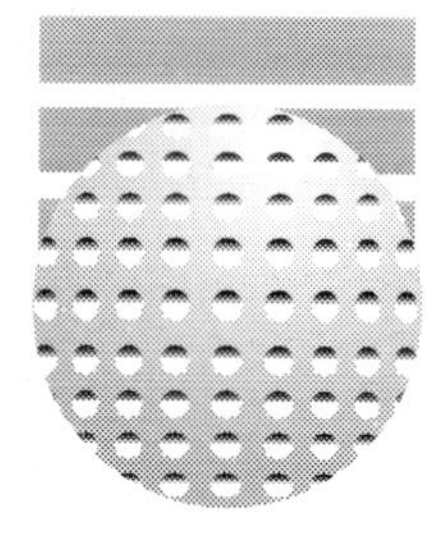

wooden cross. The last five holes present a tough finish, not least the 464-yard par four 15th and the 172-yard 17th, played into an amphitheatre of mature trees which adorn the whole course.

The 18th is a gentle finisher at under 400 yards, but again tall trees may interfere with the approach.

As one would imagine with a course of such standing, Castle Eden has produced a number of top quality players. Bill Riddell, George Olaman and Graham Border have all made a significant impact on amateur golf in the area.

Border, one of five green staff at the club, recently overhauled Olaman by winning the club championship for a record tenth time.

He has represented Durham at junior and senior level as well as being a stalwart member of the Teesside Union team for many years. Olaman has taken a leading role in golf administration and was Durham president in 1989. Dick Derby, another former category one player, was also rewarded for his commitment to golf in the area by being made president of the Teesside Union. Border replaced David Crocher as head greenkeeper in the Spring of 1994 continuing a tradition after Gordon White, a much revered character whose father also held the position of pro greenkeeper for many years. The club pride themselves on moving with the times, an example of which is their course closed sign – which also appears in Japanese. That's thanks to one T Komari, Tommy to his friends, who won the third division championship a couple of years ago before returning to his native Japan.

Castle Eden is an excellent test of golf, and despite being physically demanding in places, the scenery and setting make it well worth a visit.

It is also a friendly, affable club with fine food available and, as you might have guessed, some fine ale too!

FACTFILE

Address: Castle Eden and Peterlee Golf Club, Castle Eden, Hartlepool.

Telephone: (01429) 836220

How to get there: Follow signs to Castle Eden on Durham to Hartlepool off A19. Course opposite Whitbread brewery

Green Fees: Weekdays £20; weekends £30

Course length: 6,262

SSS: 70

Hobson Municipal Golf Club

Address: Near Burnopfield, Newcastle upon Tyne

Telephone: (01207) 271605)

How to get there: On the main A692 Consett to Gateshead road opposite Hobson industrial estate.

Course length: 6,500 yards, 18 holes

SSS: 71

Special features: The fifth is a long par 4 with a ditch on the driving area followed by a two-tier green surrounded by bunkers.

Founded: 1979.

Visitors: Welcome any time during the week. Booking necessary at weekends.

Green fees: Weekday £9, juniors and senior citizens £6; weekend £11.50.

Special packages: Can be arranged on booking.

Hotels: There are no links with hotels but accommodation can be arranged if necessary.

Woodham Golf and Country Club

Address: Burnhill Way, Newton Aycliffe, Co Durham.

Telephone: (01325) 318346

How to get there: The club is just off the A1 to Rushyford. At the Eden Arms Hotel turn left at the roundabout, go straight over the second roundabout and the golf course is on the next left.

Course length: White 6,771 yards, yellow 6,174 yards, 18 holes

SSS: 72

Special features: Probably one of the hardest course in the area.

Founded: 1984

Visitors: Welcome at all times.

Green fees: Weekdays £15 round, £20 day. Weekends £20 round.

Hotels: Old Manor House Hotel, Bishop Auckland, Redworth Hall, Eden Arms Hotel.

Further information: Has a well stocked pro shop. Male and female changing rooms, restaurant which caters for large parties if necessary.

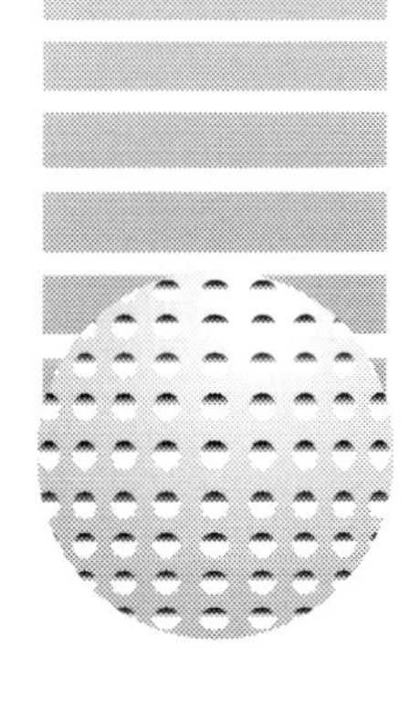

Consett Golf Club

PHILEAS Fogg would have been hard-pushed to find a more beautiful view from any golf clubhouse than that at Consett.

The hero of Jules Verne's Round the World in 80 Days now lends his name to the heavily-advertised snacks produced in Consett.

It may well be the snacks produced here that are the best known product of Consett since the steelworks disappeared. Certainly there are few people who have not been struck by the original and amusing adverts – but it is the golf course which offers a real feast.

Looking North over the Derwent Valley to the Cheviot Hills, the clubhouse offers views of 11 greens, backed by a panorama made all the more picturesque by the demolition of the iron works following its closure in 1981.

The steel workers used to have a few pence a week taken out of their wages to cover the cost of their golf fees, and after the works closed the club struggled for a couple of years to maintain its membership.

Those might have been difficult times – but the club bounced back. The boom in interest in golf which began in the mid-Eighties meant that by late 1993 there were over 200 hopefuls on the waiting list.

It is not hard to see the attraction of Consett. The parkland layout, which boasts superb greens, is played across the north-facing Elm Park Estate, which is studded with mixed woodland.

Some of the views from up here are quite spectacular and make an ideal setting for the golfer who likes a panorama to aim at.

And it's not just the views which are splendid. The course is something of a treasure as well.

The first four holes give little indication of what lies ahead. Three quite generous par fours are followed by a mild par five, all relying on the undulating terrain as their main line of defence.

Then the real test begins. The fifth and sixth, both par threes, give the first indication of the intriguing nature of the course, with par being no foregone conclusion despite their humble yardage.

The seventh is the signature hole, although it is only just long enough for a par five at 480 yards. The tee-shot is played from an elevated tee to a landing area 100 feet below. The perfect line is over the corner of a woodland with out of bounds to the

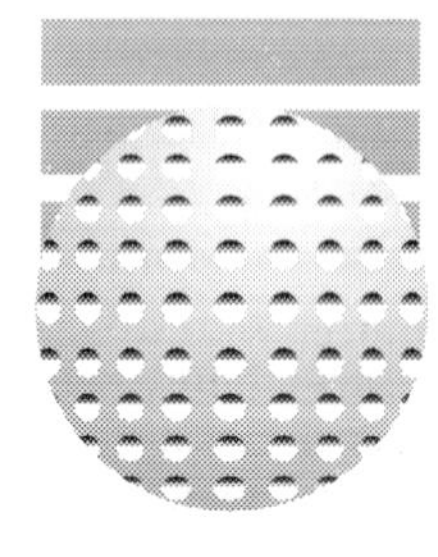

Consett Golf Course

left and a plantation awaiting the bail-out shot to the right:

The green is well protected by large trees to the left and a gathering bunker tantalisingly placed short and right of the putting surface.

The eighth is an excellent 182-yard par three alongside the masked grounds of Shotley Bridge Hospital, while the tee-shot at the par five ninth requires arrow-like accuracy to cling to the path hewn through towering pines.

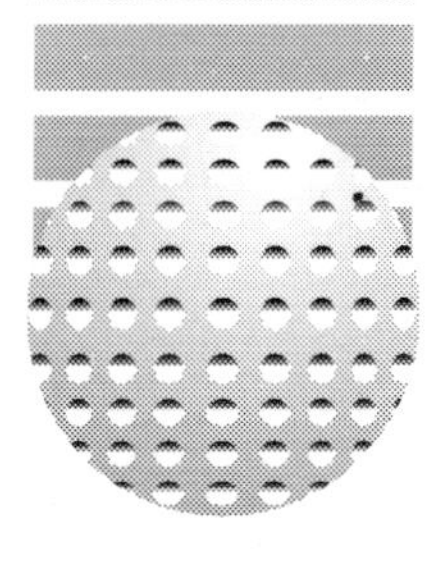

Consett Golf Club

The big hitters may be tempted to go for the green in two here. It could be a dangerous temptation. The fairway rises steeply to a two-tiered green with varying degrees of danger either side.

The second half begins with a reachable par five, the green providing all manner of problems as it slopes sharply from right to left.

Heartbreak Hill is the adopted name of the 15th, coming so late as it does in the round. This can be a real tough one to conquer. Establishing base camp on the fairway is a must, the approach shot requiring pinpoint accuracy as the green is cut into a shelf on the bank side with anything wayward being thrown off line.

It is just the sort of challenge which creeps up on unwary golfers taking a breather.

The 16th, a mild par four, and the 17th, a short par three, hold no respite for the complacent, while the last hole is driveable once a large hillock is negotiated in the fairway.

Otherwise a tricky blind approach shot from below the level of the green is almost guaranteed.

One of the reasons the 18th is such a test is because keeping your eye on the ball is tough as competition comes from some quite stunning views. Many a player will have paused here after holing out to take a last look at what can be a truly inspiring series of views.

And then comes the 19th. Here, too, Consett, as you would expect, provides a really pleasant and friendly atmosphere. Rounding off what is always an enjoyable outing.

Phileas Fogg doesn't know what he missed...

FACTFILE

Address: Consett and District Golf Club, Elmfield Road, Consett, Co Durham.

Telephone: (01207) 502186

How to get there: Twelve miles from Durham (A691) and Newcastle (A694). Off A68 two miles from

Green Fees: Weekdays £15; weekends £20 (visitors welcome after 9.30am but call first to check availability.

Course length: 6,013

SSS: 69

Other information: The 15th is nicknamed Heartbreak Hill because of the steep upwards climb.

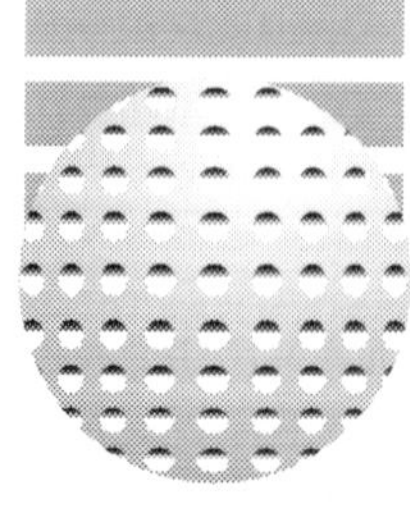

View from the clubhouse at Consett Golf Club

View over Beamish Park Golf Club

Beamish Park Golf Club

BEAMISH Park Golf Club, adjacent to the award-winning museum, is a beautiful parkland course set amid rolling forested hills.

From the 12th hole onwards it is especially memorable, with the 15th taking pride of place because of its daunting elevated tee-shot down a narrow wooded valley.

Directions to the course sound as if they have come straight out of a Lewis Carrol yarn: 'Head towards Stanley, turn right when you get to No Place and left when you see the museum's double-decker trams.'

The course certainly possesses a magic of its own. Even the central character of that well-loved nursery rhyme Bobby Shafto had his part to play in the course's existence, with his family home serving as the clubhouse for many years.

The Shafto family, who dominated the local mining industry in the early part of the century, certainly left a fitting pile to overlook the course, which was designed on the estate's deer park and fine-tuned in the Sixties by Henry Cotton.

The clubhouse was built in 1973 and updated in 1992 with £180,000 being spent on a new locker room and showers plus a beautifully refurbished bar.

The club has had a stormy relationship with the museum, which began when they earmarked Holme Farm for their clubhouse. The museum objected because of the architectural value of a chimney attached to the farm buildings. The claim was upheld and the farm now forms part of the museum's many attractions.

Another battle with the museum forced the club to relocate their original first hole, a tremendous par three from an elevated tee played to a green 200 yards away in the valley bottom. Shots sliced over the wall to the right found their way into the museum car park and with more than 1,000 balls being recovered as evidence the hole was ruled out of bounds.

The new first hole and the 17th run along the valley bottom, separated from the Shafto Hall rhodedendrons by a stream and a wall. There is also a beck running across the fairways, ready to catch an errant second at the first, which is an unforgiving 527 yards.

The second is a modest 323 yards with a blind second shot to a two-tiered green, while the third is a 200-yard, well bunkered par three. The fourth, or dip as it is named on the

Beamish Museum from the 1st tee at Beamish Golf Club

card, is not for the faint-hearted. At 448 yards, it is one of the toughest par fours in Durham because of the huge hollow in front of the green.

The uphill drive must reach the brow of the hill to allow any attempt at the green, with the second shot needing to carry the full distance over 200 yards to stand any chance of reaching the putting surface. The seventh bends subtly to the right and the perfect tee-shot will fade gently into the gap in the trees to leave a short pitch to the sunken green surrounded by overhanging trees. An iron off the

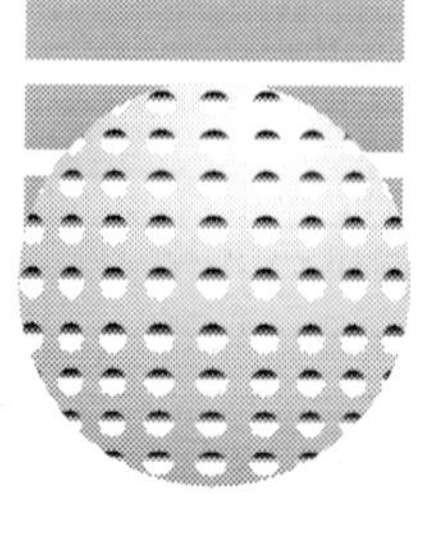

tee will be many people's choice here. The 12th is another tough par four at 465 yards, although it is downhill.

A classic dogleg left, with Penshaw Monument providing the marker for the long-sighted, it has two natural ponds awaiting ambitious attempts to cut off the corner. The ponds also play their part on the uphill 14th, which will require your best two shots to achieve a regulation four.

The 374-yard 15th is undoubtedly the most nerve-wracking hole. The fairway is only 20 yards wide at one point and with accuracy more important than distance many prefer an iron from the tee. Position is paramount as several trees overhang the assault on the green, and the hole certainly brings the best out of the thinking golfer.

The 16th is a cheeky little hole at 150 yards, with a tee shot out of the trees to a sunken green hiding behind two imposing bunkers. The last hole or 'Home climb' is under 300 yards. However, the ascent leaves many hoping there will be oxygen on draught at the 19th.

The club has produced a number of top amateurs, the most famous being double county matchplay champion Bobby Hindhaugh, one of only a handful of players to represent Durham on 50 occasions. Professional Chris Cole has been at the club since 1986 after serving his apprenticeship under his father Malcolm at Hartlepool.

There is a warm welcome in the clubhouse with lunchtime snacks providing excellent value, with a la carte meals on request. Hopefully there will be no more wrangles with the museum, as there are obvious mutual benefits of a harmonious existence. A classic case of something for all the family.

FACTFILE

Address: Beamish Park Golf Club, Beamish, Stanley, Co Durham

Telephone: (0191) 370 1982

How to get there: Take Chester-le-Street turnoff off the A1(m) follow signs to Beamish Museum

Green Fees: weekdays £16 round, £20 day.

Course length: 6,205 yards

SSS: 70

Special deals: Reduced fees for parties of 40 or more.

Other information: Clubhouse recently renovated to high standard.

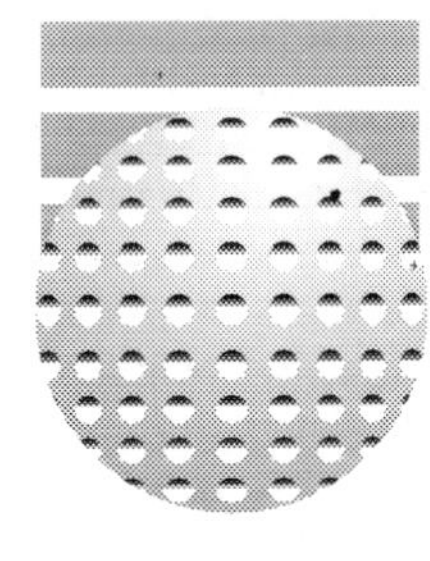

Wearside Golf Club

THE first inviting glimpse of Wearside Golf Course, in the shadow of Penshaw Monument, is spied from the elevated track which makes its way to the clubhouse and serves as a mouth-watering curtain-raiser to a rich golfing experience.

It is difficult to believe once you have arrived at the modern pavilion that less than two minutes ago you had been fighting the contraflow on the A19 which is mercifully cloaked from the course by the surrounding countryside.

Peter Sutton, club captain in 1991, was responsible for producing one of the most stylish and comprehensive centenary publications around although his research was hampered by clubhouse fires in 1909 and 1956 which destroyed valuable records.

The fires also took their toll on players' equipment. One such unfortunate was Peter Inman. A dermatologist by profession he gained the nickname 'Inman the Skinman' and was known for buying a putter whenever he felt the one he was using was misbehaving.

The abandoned putters were dispatched to his locker. The look on the insurance assessor's face when the Skinman submitted a claim for 'shoes, bag, set of clubs and 19 putters' must have been a sight to behold.

The construction of the first nine-hole course in 1893 on the current site was overseen by T Carruthers of Edinburgh and was increased to 18 after the club sought advice from the legendary Harry Vardon following his visit in 1899.

The layout was enhanced in 1926 when Harry S Colt was commissioned to 'increase players' interest without making the course unduly strenuous'.

A course record 65 in 1928 by Newcastle's Cyril Fryer confirmed that Colt had fulfilled his brief.

Wearside is one of that rare breed of courses which has a par-three opener, a tricky 172 yards off the back tees with a sloping green. Out of bounds right provides the main obstacle at the 371-yard par-four second where the wayward opener is punished, a fate which awaits the incurable slicer again down the third and fourth.

The fifth is a monstrous par five at 570 yards eased only by its descent to a green which slopes steeply away from the front while backing onto the riverbank.

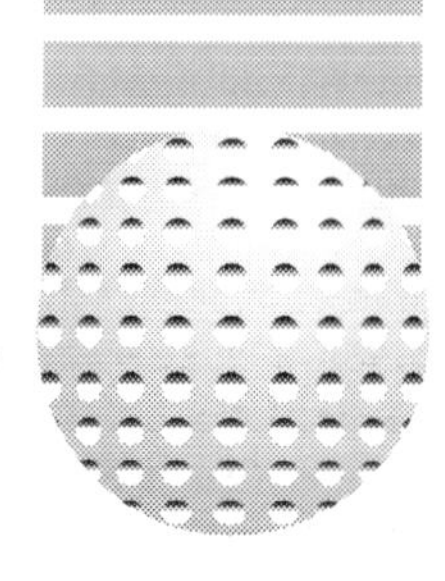

Wearside Golf Club

The sixth is the first of a trio of classic holes at 400 yards. The tee shot is played blind from below the level of the fairway which runs away to the river on the right, while semi-mature trees to the left provide more than a token hindrance.

The line from the tee is Penshaw Monument, a replica Grecian Temple of Theseus built to commemorate John George Lambton Earl of Durham. During a club pro-am some years ago Peter Tupling, professional at Boldon, inquired about the line, to which his playing partners replied the ideal line was the momument. Perfectionist Tupling replied: 'Which column?'

The approach shot to the sixth is no pushover. A severe hollow on the right fringe leads to out of bounds, while a ravine awaits the ambitious.

The seventh is guaranteed to get the pulse pumping – a par three which requires a carry of all but 20 of its 160 yards.

Out of bounds acts as a magnet down the right while the safe route left is protected by bunkers.

Eight and nine are medium par fours while the second half begins with a demanding 390-yard two-shotter, a water hazard waiting in front of the green.

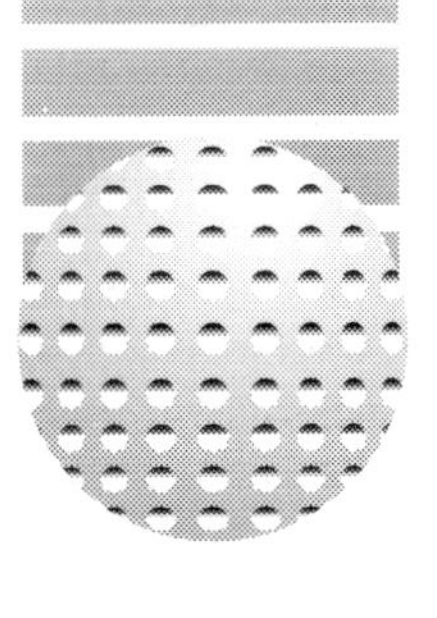

The 13th and 14th are at opposite ends of the par-three spectrum. The 13th at 224 yards is at best a long iron while the 14th is a mirror image of the seventh.

Holes 15 and 17 allow mild respite at just over 300 yards while 16 and 18 eat into the reserves of concentration and must be treated with utmost caution.

In 1990 Wearside juniors won all four major county championship titles. Richard Walker won the Durham stroke play while Howard Walton won the matchplay equivalent. Billy Edgar and David Guest won the junior stroke and matchplay titles respectively. Encouragement for bright young prospects is never far away from the older players who have performed at the highest level in County golf. John Naisby followed up his 1974 victory in the county matchplay championship by collecting the stroke play title in 1977 and 1979, while Jackie Sanderson, Durham champion in 1962, has been elected captain of the North Durham Union.

Duncan Wood, the Tyne Tees Television presenter, won the Durham matchplay title in 1986, while stalwarts such as Dougie Bell, Bob Turner, David Goss and Les Storey give the club a formidable depth of experience.

Wearside has also produced a string of dedicated administrators including Frank Boulton, county treasurer for countless members until his death a couple of years ago.

The most recent appointment onto the County executive is 1993 captain Graham Hope, who has taken over as competition secretary, replacing John Walker now with the E.G.U.

The future as very bright for this most concientious of clubs and I left with an overwhelming belief that in the words of P G Wodehouse that 'one instinctively knows when something is right.'

FACTFILE

Address: Wearside Golf Club, Coxgreen, Sunderland, Tyne and Wear.

Telephone: (0191) 534 2518

How to get there: Take A183 towards Chester-le-Street from the A19, after 400 yeards turn right at Coxgreen sign, left at T-junction.

Green Fees: Weekdays £24; weekends £30

Course length: 6,373

SSS: 70

Special deals: Reduction on fees for parties of 12-plus and on catering.

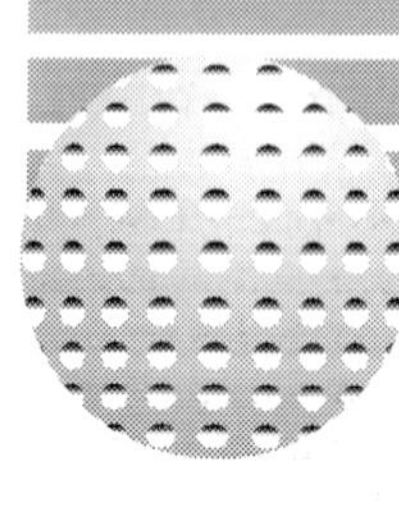

Durham City Golf Club

SITUATED on the banks of the meandering River Browney at Littleburn, this is a classic example of the old making way for the new.

The current course, which has seen a vast improvement in recent years under the watchful eye of course manager Stan Shotton, celebrated its 20th anniversary in 1994.

But the club itself was one of the first to be formed in the area, as a modest sixholer in 1887 at the delightfully named Pinkerknowle.

The course was extended to nine holes in 1893 and in 1928 the club obtained a 25-year lease on a 90-acre site at nearby Mount Oswald and formed the Durham City Golf Club Ltd.

Unsuccessful attempts to buy the land and the subsequent protracted negotiations with various landlords meant that peace of mind for the future of the club was never achieved. Concern grew further when the course was excluded from designated greenbelt provisions in the mid-Sixties.

In October 1969, the 100-acre site at Littleburn was bought for £27,500 with the help of interest-free loans from the members, finally securing a permanent home in 1974.

A few alterations have been made to the initial layout, the most notable being the extension by 100 yards of the sixth hole and the creation of a new par three seventh. Both are excellent holes, designed by the original course architect, club member Chris Stanton.

The 423-yard sixth has the river along its full length to the right and a line of bunkers flanking the left at driving length. The seventh is only 140 yards but has a postage stamp green nestling among a spinney of silver birches.

The maturing trees play an important role in bringing the river into play, significantly on the third and fourth, both of which are par fours in excess of 400 yards.

Add to this a 500-yard plus opener, and the notorious sloping green at the par three second, and the first six holes certainly sort out the men from the boys.

A large pond at the left of the 355-yard dog-leg tenth plants seeds of doubt as well as adding to the aesthetic appeal of the hole, while a ravine at the 523-yard 11th prevents all but the biggest hitters getting up in two.

The 13th was the stroke index one hole before the extension to the sixth, possibly because concentration

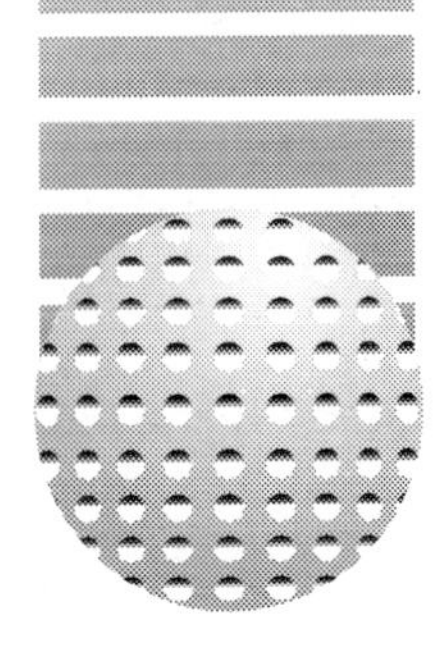

Durham City Golf Club

The 7th green at Durham City

is often broken by the constant stream of InterCity 125s on the railway line to the left.

The well-defined par five 14th, protected by trees of all shapes and sizes, is reachable in two at 485 yards. But a bunker short and right acts as a magnet. Like the par three second, the 174-yard 15th has a green sloping from back to front and the art is to finish short of the hole.

Contrasting dog-legs follow at 16 and 17. The tempting short cut at the former is protected by a large bunker. The latter leaves the player with no option but to lay up with an iron off the tee before sizing up a well-bunkered green. The 18th is a relatively straightforward two-shotter at 337 yards to a green which provides the opportunity for a

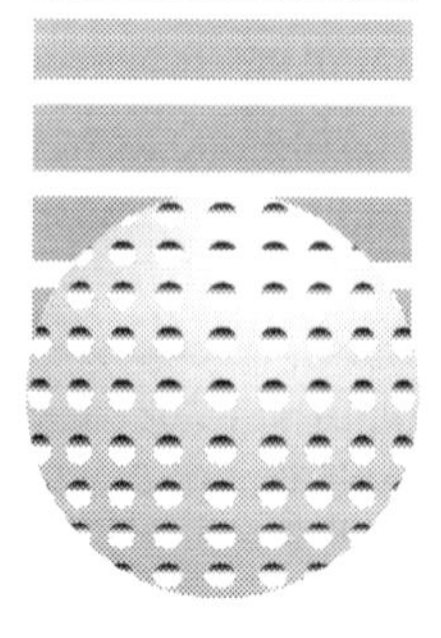

grandstand finish as it is overlooked by the clubhouse balcony.

Two of Durham City's longest standing and conscientious members were chosen as captains during centenary year. It meant a third term for Arthur Parkin, who has served on the committee for over 30 years, several of those as chairman.

Although the club has had limited team success, no doubt a by-product of the earlier uncertainty, individual honours have been earned by a number of members. Stuart Neil has been a county regular for a number of years and won the area's Club Champion of Champions tournament when the event was held at his home club in centenary year.

Martin Sexton and Alan Ramshaw have also had outside success, while Bobby Green, Alan Doxford, Ken Saint and Geoff Charlton, who learned their golf at the City, have gained success at pastures new.

FACTFILE

Address: Durham City Golf Club, Littleburn, Langley Moor, Co Durham.

Telephone: (0191) 378069

How to get there: Off A690 two miles south west of Durham City

Green Fees: Weekdays £18; weekends £24 (check for availability at weekends)

Course length: 6,326

SSS: 70

Other information: Clubhouse extension planned

The club has a refreshing approach to junior golf. A combined effort between junior liaison officer Dave Shillito, professional Steve Corbally and club steward Alan Lyle has reaped dividends with the club boasting over a dozen single figure youngsters.

The committee has recently approved the provision of a purpose-built shop to be incorporated into the clubhouse.

Lyle and wife Sue, previously at the Bonny Moorhen in Stanhope, have taken to golf club life admirably. Alan is a keen golfer and is given priority tee times in competitions to ensure he is back in time to pull a mean pint of Theakston's and assist Anne in providing a varied and mouth-watering array of traditional home-made fare.

Durham has an uncanny air of friendliness with all sections catered for by a club which seems to thrive on harmony.

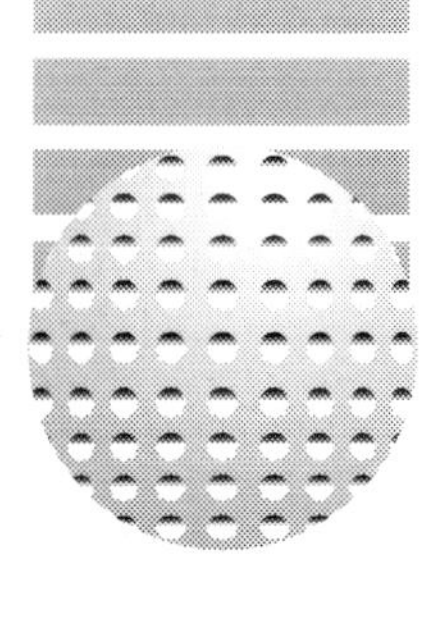

Knotty Hill Golf Club

SEDGEFIELD farmer Denis Craggs took the bull by the horns, while many others were left in the starting stalls.

In 1984 there were some 1,800 planning approvals for new golf courses in England, but most had got no further than the drawing board.

Craggs' project at Knotty Hill Golf Centre, near Hardwick Hall Hotel, becomes ever more ambitious.

Having opened a fully-equipped floodlit driving range in 1991, he has now opened an 18-hole course and has been granted approval for a further 18 holes which he hopes to bring to championship standard to sit alongside the beginners' course already in use.

While other farmers seeking to follow advice to diversify developed feet as cold as the economic climate, Craggs and his staff of four worked round the clock to meet their vision.

'People ask me how we could build a course during a recession while they had planning permission but could-not get started,' he said.

'The answer is that we have a natural site. The only earth moving we did was in shaping the greens, and we have everything on site that we needed to build the course.

'We won't have to bring any materials in for 50 years. We will even top dress the greens with what we have on site.

'And the drainage is so good we've been able to stay open all the time during the recent heavy rain. You could travel the country and not find another site like this.'

Craggs, who has never played golf, travelled extensively looking at courses new and old, talking to greenkeepers and seeking golfers' advice before drawing up his plans. He and his team then built the course themselves. I told them it would be hard work,' he said. 'I said I had deadlines to meet and if they didn't think they were up to it they should say so. We worked from 7am to 10pm seven days a week for 16 months without a break, and there was never a cross word.'

Admittedly, not all of that time was spent on the course, as Craggs still had to run his farm and small haulage business to keep the money coming in.

Although there are a few nicely constructed ponds, including one in front of the first tee, this will remain

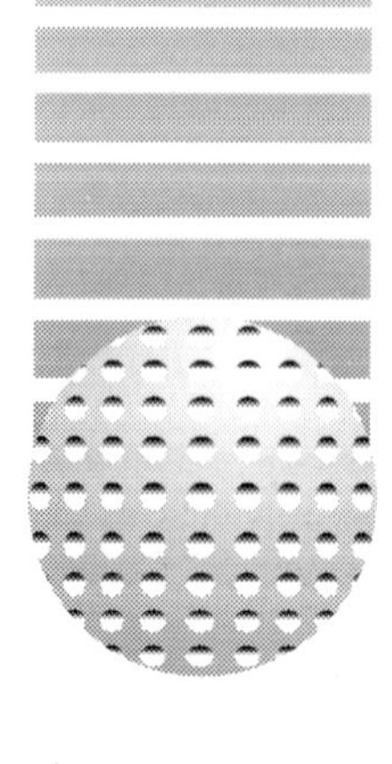

Splashing out of a bunker

a course built with the beginner in mind, with wide fairways.

'There is nothing worse when someone is learning the game than to be searching for balls all round the course,' said Craggs.

Many good golf course layouts have been spoilt by poor greens, but Craggs has taken advice on this subject from every conceivable authority.

With the help of former Durham secretary Bill Murray, the chairman of the EGU course development committee, the greens are laid to USGA standards.

Craggs acquired the irrigation system from the Gateshead Garden Festival, and visited the site of the Welsh Festival at Ebbw Vale to buy more irrigation equipment.

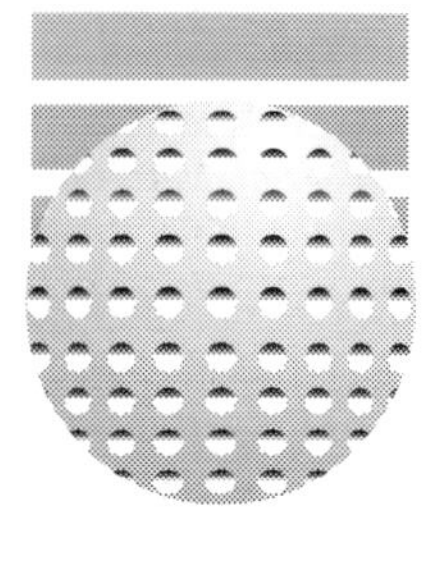

He hopes ultimately to have the watering controlled from a computerised pump house.

Nick Todd, the son of former Darlington professional Ian Todd, helps to run the shop and the driving range, which is open from 8am to 9pm seven days a week. Craggs's sister, Judith Reynolds, completes the hard-working and friendly team, acting as secretary and liaison officer.

So far 210 acres of farmland are committed to the project and the plans are well underway for a par 73 course, measuring 7,300 yards.

"We wanted to see if we had room for a big, challenging course. But we will have to scale it down a bit," said Craggs.

Some of the holes would be cut into woodland, with the trees being transplanted to the existing course.

The owner says he is concentrating on a second course ahead of a clubhouse because that's what the members want.

FACTFILE

Address: Knotty Hill, Sedgefield, Stockton-on-Tees TS21 2BB

Telephone: (01740) 20320

How to get there: Two miles off A1(m) on the A689 Teesside Road

Course length: 6,700

Par: 73

Green fees: On application

And he has been told by the council it is such a good site that when he does build a clubhouse it should be something of architectural merit.

Meanwhile, well-furnished portable cabins provide adequate office, shop and changing facilities, and it is intended to provide a permanent marquee for catering purposes.

It's a prime site in more ways than one, in that most of the surrounding clubs have waiting lists running into three figures and people are jumping at the chance to use Knotty Hill as their starting point on the road to Faldo-like fame.

Although these are early days for one of Durham's newest golf courses, it seems farmer Craggs has backed a winner.

Being on the course at Sedgefield doesn't mean losing money on the horses.

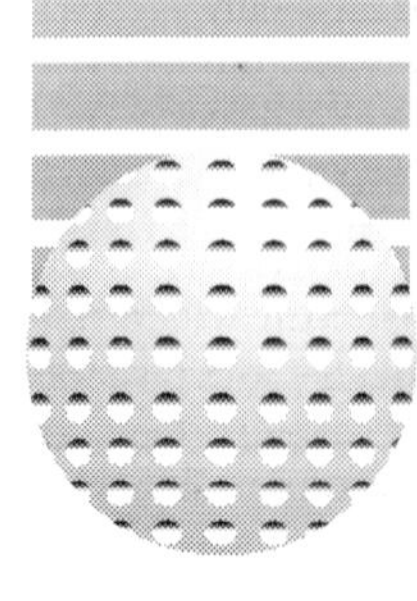

Hall Garth Golf Club

WHAT promises to be one of the most spectacular par 3 holes in the North-East is taking excellent shape at a new golf course just outside Darlington.

Work began just before Christmas 1992 on a nine-hole course at Hall Garth Hotel, Coatham Mundeville, and, despite some teething troubles following an official opening, the course will be in full swing by Spring 1995.

The hole is a 165-yard par three up a narrow avenue of trees, with a stream and a lake down the right and a bank at the back of the green.

It looks a frightening prospect for players of all abilities, but the hole's aesthetic appeal and the challenge it presents will have visitors itching to get round the nine holes and try it again.

It's the only par three on a 3,500-yard lay-out which includes two par fives and six par fours, mostly over 400 yards.

Another challenging hole is the par five sixth, where both the tee-shot and the approach are over bends in the meandering River Skerne. Three bunkers await anyone trying to take a safe route.

The course was designed by Bryan Moor, of OCM Associates, a former Yorkshire hockey captain whose brother Tony kept goal for Darlington and captained Scarborough cricket team to three national knock-out cup victories at Lord's.

Scarborough-born, he also played cricket for Yorkshire seconds as a team-mate of Dickie Bird. Now off seven handicap at Southerness in South-West Scotland, at his best he played off four.

He learnt the game at Scarborough North Cliff before becoming secretary at Thetford Golf Club in Norfolk in 1980.

He moved on to Sundridge Park in Kent, and it was there that he became interested in course design after previously working for 30 years as ice cream sales manager for Lyons.

'We had several quotes in for three greens to be revamped because of flooding,' he said. 'That was in 1986 and the estimates were around £20,000.

'My partner and I took the job in hand and finally got the whole problem solved for £3,500. That was what got me started. We try to build golf courses that people can afford. When the boom started everybody was talking in millions.

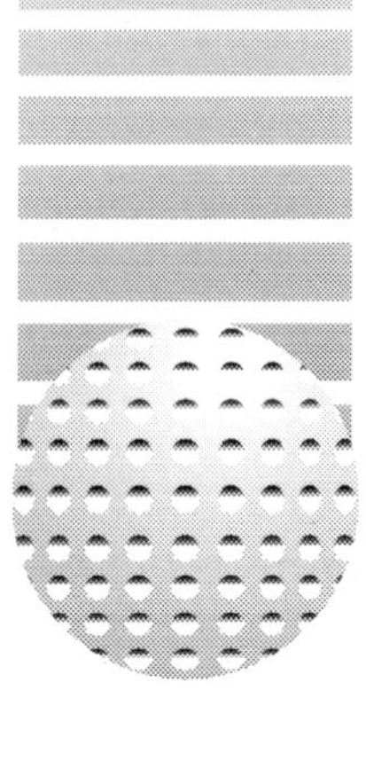

Hall Garth Golf Club

Hall Garth – should be ready for players in Spring 1995

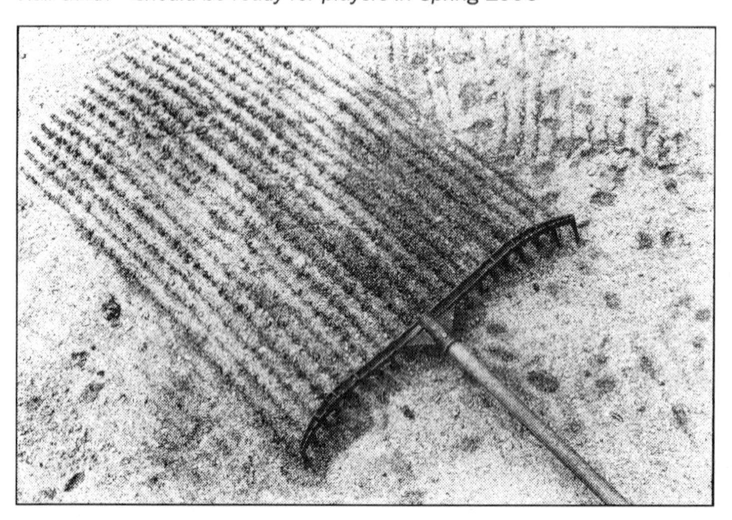

'I couldn't build something like Jack Nicklaus''s course at St Mellion. To me it's loud and vulgar.

'In cases like that you are paying for muck-shifting, creating something that isn't there. We try to make the most of the natural landscape.'

Even though greens were built to the highest specifications, Bryan estimates the cost of building Hall Garth's nine holes did not exceed £130,00.

That includes £30,000 on 2,500 tons of top-quality root zone for the greens, which was been brought in from the Wirral. A further £22,000 was spent on irrigation for the tees and greens.

Five lakes have been created and a lot of surgery has been done on existing trees, including oak and copper beech, while new ones are being planted.

The 68-acre site, formerly a mixture of rough pasture and arable, was

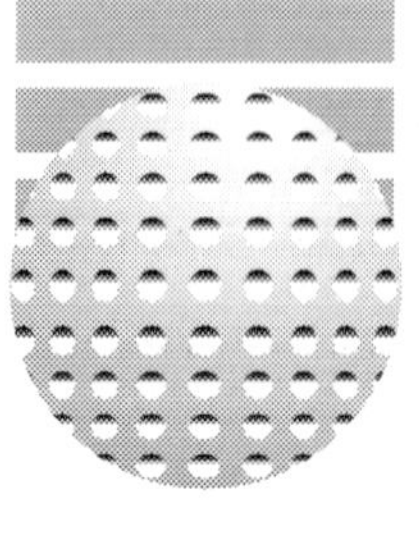

bought from a local doctor by Hall Garth's former owner John Forbes.

A 20-handicap member of Thirsk and Northallerton, he bought the four-star country manor hotel in 1988 and extended it to 40 bedrooms.

Forbes had to endure a two-year planning wrangle after his lengthy negotiations to buy the land.

'Councils encourage you to extend and create jobs, then put every possible obstacle in your way,' he said.

'There's a deer house on the land which has been there since 1720. Nobody has ever done anything with it, but it's a listed building and we were told we had to renovate it.

'We also had to reduce the fifth from a par five to a par four because of a footpath across the land which I have never seen anyone use. We had a long battle with the Ramblers' Association over that.

'But once everything was agreed the council were over the moon with the course. They think it's wonderful.'

Bryan Moor is also clearly excited by the development, despite having to change his plans twice. The biggest disappointment was being prevented by the River Authority from building a green in a perfect loop of the river.

But most of the greens are close to water and present attractive targets.

Three green staff were appointed to work on the project from the outset, and the head greenkeeper is James Webster, formerly at Eaglescliffe, Darlington and Bishop Auckland.

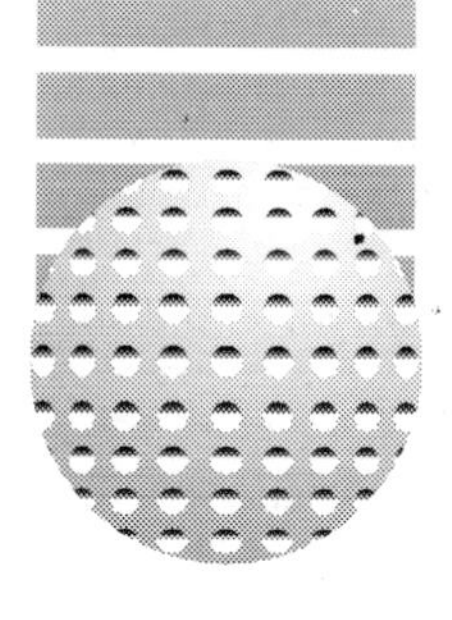

South Moor Golf Club

DEEP in North-West Durham lies a hidden gem among the county's golf courses. Against a backdrop of Stanley's terraced houses and on land owned by the Coal Board, South Moor presents a surprisingly picturesque and undeniably challenging course.

It's very much a case of 'once driven forever smitten' as the moorland terrain offers fine views, undulating fairways and excellent greens designed by renowned course architect Dr Alister Mackenzie.

Heather and gorse add to the delights in an area which could yet face further blight from open-cast mining. But while Coal Industry Estates continue to resist the club's attempts to buy the land, the cloud cast by Old King Coal could turn out to have a silver lining from a new mining venture.

Mining firm R and A Young wants to open-cast a 55-acre site adjacent to the course, and there is every chance it would then be turned over to the club. 'That would give us space for an extra nine holes, which would be wonderful,' says club secretary Brian Davison.

'The mining would only last for six months. They want to drain their site through our land, and we are trying to do a deal with them so that we get the land when they have finished with it.'

Meanwhile the battle to buy the existing land goes on. 'The club was founded in 1923 and we paid a peppercorn rent until 1976, when we were given a 42-year lease,' said Davison. 'Now the rent is £7,500 a year. We have been negotiating for two years to buy the land, and have even written to the chairman of the Coal Board and to our MP, Giles Radice. But we're not making much progress.'

The ever improving infertile land, with its shallow top soil, has meant that the club has suffered drainage problems in the past. A five-year improvement plan began in 1989, and with the green staff being increased from two to five great strides have been made. There have also been changes behind the scenes from the time when the committee had to be chosen from Coal Board members.

Now all committee members are golfers, and the course improvements they have instituted, even down to fine details such as feeding the heather, have seen a dramatic turnaround. Membership is now full

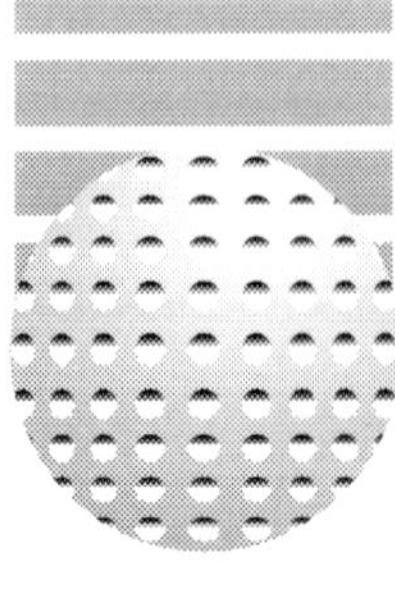

The 18th hole at South Moor – view from the tee

The 13th hole at Ravensworth Golf Club

Teeing off at the 6th at South Moor

at 650, with the waiting list closed at 100.

The course has an unusual start with a par three followed by a 477-yard par five and another par three, measuring 153 yards to a green delightfully situated in the edge of a mature woodland. The course then reverts to a more conventional format with six straight par fours, the most notable of which is the ninth. Played from a sunken tee, the fairway is flanked by heather and gorse and leads to a basin green. The prevailing wind usually makes the hole play much more than its 406 yards.

The 12th earns the stroke index one title because of its tight drive and

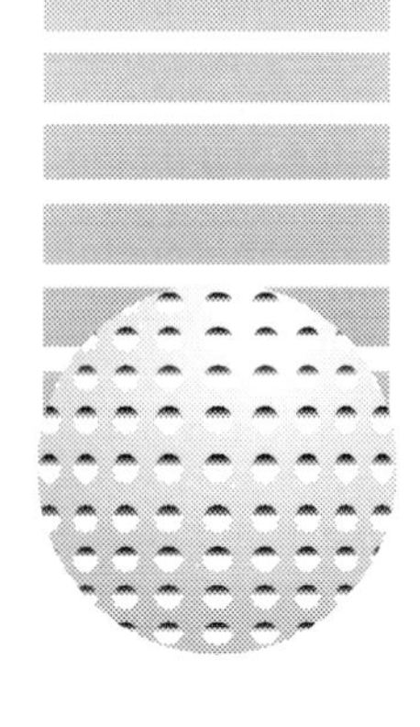

South Moor Golf Club

blind uphill second shot to a plateau fairway, which is protected to the right by the course's boundary wall. Another feature hole is the 16th, which is a sheer dogleg with a brook at the corner and trees waiting to ensnare those who attempt the direct route.

While the course may be unfamiliar with the rank and file of golfers, the sons, and latterly daughters, of this golfing outpost certainly are not.

One of the great stalwarts is Roy Clark, who until 1991 was only the second player in the history of Durham golf to have won the county strokeplay and matchplay titles in the same year. Another South Moor product, Jackie Ord, won the Durham strokeplay championship twice.

More recently Jim Handy has been a regular county player while Pauline Dobson has won the county ladies' title on more than one occasion.

FACTFILE

Address: South Moor Golf Club, The Middles, Craghead, Stanley, Co Durham.

Telephone: (01207) 232848

How to get there: Four and a half miles west of Chester-le-Street, one mile south of Stanley west of B6313 South Moor to Durham road

Course length: 6,445

SSS: 71

Green Fees: Weekdays £21 for day, £14 per round; weekends £25

Special deals: £1 reduction for parties of 20 or over; deals available on catering.

The clubhouse atmosphere is akin to a friendly working men's club, a function it fulfilled for many years because of the mining influence. The club maintains an air of fun and a fellowship which was personified when the club embarked upon a fundraising night-time golf event in the form of a Texas scramble played with torches and illuminated balls.

Such was members' generosity that £23,000 was raised for Children in Need.

If you enjoy a good test of your golf, excellent greens and a warm welcome at the 19th, the hidden delights of South Moor are well worth exploring.

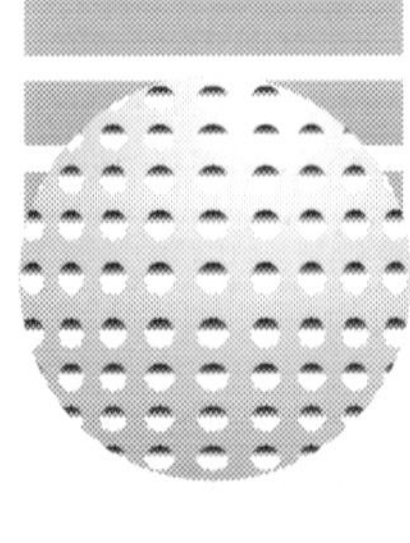

Ravensworth Golf Club

A COURSE perched on top of a hill surrounded by housing estates and containing a number of quirky holes seems an unlikely setting for one of the most prolific providers of Durham County golfers.

Ravensworth, situated on the outskirts of Gateshead, has stood the test of time since 1906, refusing to surrender to the assault from all sides of bricks and mortar.

Conversely, the views afforded by its highest points compare favourably with the panorama you would expect when stepping off a ski lift in late spring. The clubhouse is testament to this renowned drinking parish where, for many, pints and putts receive equal billing.

Yet the club has won more county honours over the years than almost any club in the area, having lifted the Durham Clubs' Championship title no fewer than 17 times.

At 5,872 yards the par of 68 is matched by the standard scratch, but in the words of many a football manager it is definitely a game of two halves.

Despite having equal par totals of 34, the front nine is over 500 yards longer, containing two very demanding par fours of over 450 yards, the second and the ninth.

After a gentle 305-yard opener the second, at 475 yards, requires brute force with no room for ignorance. An elevated drive leaves a daunting blind second shot over a pair of fairway bunkers to a landing area flanked by gorse, giving the hole almost a links feel.

With out-of-bounds lurking to the left and back, anything less than a double bogey here is a bonus. The third is a drive and flick hole, while the fourth, a 224-yard par three, narrows to a well-guarded green with out-of-bounds on either side.

The next five holes provide the toughest stretch on the course with four par fours, the shortest being 374 yards, plus the par three eighth, which at 243 yards directly uphill is the toughest one-shotter around.

The ninth is probably the best hole on the course. A demanding tight drive, with bungalows to the right and a dense copse to the left, is followed by a blind second shot, which requires local knowledge to find the target.

The basin-greened tenth is a classic short hole, while the 11th is the only par five on the course with a chance to grab a shot back for the home-

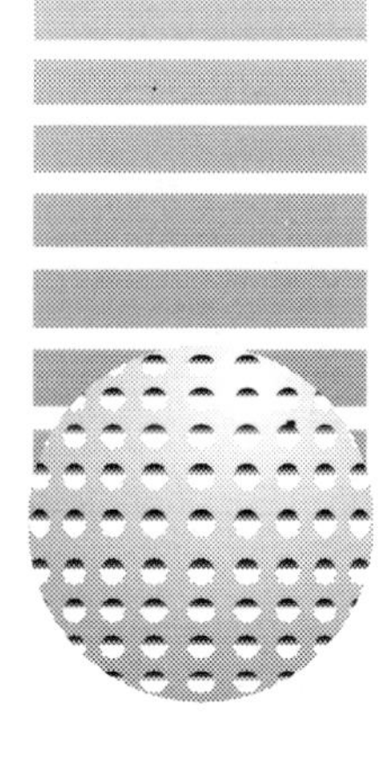

Ravensworth Golf Club

Ravensworth – more honours over the years than almost any club in the area

ward run. The par four 12th tempts the big hitters to go for the green. But plenty of danger awaits either side of the coffin-shaped green. The 13th is a superb par three played from an elevated tee to a postage-stamp green, guarded by a number of pot bunkers.

Depending on the wind the 194 yards can require anything from a driver to a wedge. Another two reachable par fours are separated by the par three 15th, at just under 200 yards a very good short hole, while the 17th awaits to punish good and bad scorers at 459 yards.

An ample landing area leaves yet another blind second shot, where an assault on the steep ridge is a must for visitors to pick out the correct line. The 18th is a classic finishing hole. It is invariably a drive and pitch, but a subtle two-tier green and the car park at the rear will sow seeds of doubt in the minds of birdie seekers.

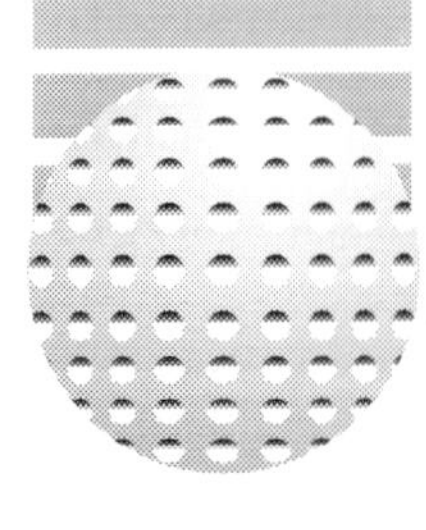

The club has one of the best amateurs in the North-East in Craig Kilgour, who achieved the double of Durham Strokeplay and Matchplay champion in 1991. He successfully defended his matchplay title the following year and continues to play a leading role in the Durham County team.

It is a tradition which goes back to the Twenties and Thirties, when Messrs Armitage and Alan Harrison figured prominently in the Durham championship. The halcyon days, however, came in the late Fifties and early Sixties, when the Wrekenton wreckers Ian Hornsby (capped over 50 times for Durham), Geoff Dixon (of Dixon Sports fame), George Bayley (Radio 5 commentator) and Brian Bolam (1988-90 county captain) monopolised team golf while also representing their county.

One of only three juniors in those days, Jim Thomas, influenced by the club's success, rose to boys international honours in 1964, teaming up with, among others, Peter Oosterhuis after winning the Durham Boys title on two occasions.

Current low handicappers include Mark Redferne, Glenn Hodges, John Thompson, renowned long-hitter Joe Jackson, and Kevin Kelly, a winner of the Ravensworth Bowl, the prestigious 36-hole open scratch event hosted by the club.

Bob Fiddler and his wife Liz have continued the tradition of good food and ale, having previously been steward and stewardess at Houghton-le-Spring. Bob, one of the rare breed of golf-playing stewards, remembers that his surname seemed especially unfortunate when he joined forces with the South Moor steward to win third prize in a Black Bottle Whisky tournament. His partner's name was Billy Crook!

FACTFILE

Address: Wrekenton, Gateshead, Tyne and Wear

Telephone: (0191) 4876014

How to get there: Two miles south of Gateshead town centre on the B1296

Course length: 5,872

SSS: 68

Founded: 1906

Visitors: Welcome at any time

Green fees: £17 per round weekdays, £25 per round weekends and Bank Holidays

Special packages: Reduced green fees, depending on size of party

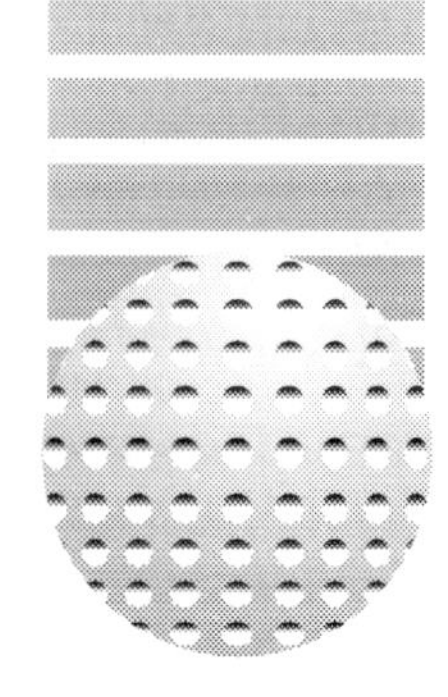

Boldon Golf Club

BOLDON is known almost as much for its professional's shop as for the quality of its course, although it did produce one of the great characters of Durham golf in Dawson Hunter.

A life member, Dawson began as a greenkeeper before the war and returned afterwards to stamp his mark on club and county golf.

In 1957 he became the first person to win the Durham strokeplay and matchplay titles in the same year and he won the club championship 13 times from 1948-75.

The professional, Richard Phipps, has one of the best-stocked golf shops in the North-East, offering a wide range of clubs at competitive prices.

Originally from Bedfordshire, his first job was as an assistant pro at Boldon, but it was at Wallsend that he established his business reputation.

After suffering five burglaries in one year, he returned to Boldon in 1987, moving into a large purpose-built shop with no windows.

He has two business partners in Sean Richardson and Philip Carlaw, while his wife Beryl also works full-time in the shop along with other assistants.

'We sell golf clubs because we are golf professionals,' said 46-year-old Phipps. 'We are not clothing specialists or experts in electric trollies.

'We offer a friendly service and even if people don't buy anything we hope they will come back.

'I hardly play these days. Certainly not as much as I'd like to, but you can't do everything.'

Richard also has a reputation as a good teacher and includes former England amateur player John Metcalfe, now a tournament professional, among his former pupils.

His brick-built shop forms a rather featureless extension of an attractive clubhouse, which was originally a large house in its own grounds.

It was bought in 1926, the same year as the course was extended from nine to 18 holes, 14 years after the club was founded.

Designed by Harry Vardon, the course is mainly meadowland but with a hint of inland links around the third and fourth.

These are both par threes featuring a quarry, plus several humps and hollows and the sort of rocky out-

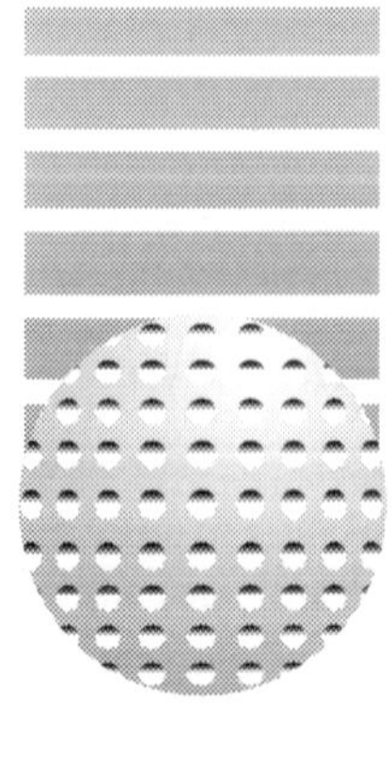

A twitchy time for spectators

crops which occur sporadically throughout the course.

Of the two opening par fours, the first offers a gentle start at 285 yards, while the second is an attractive dog-leg right with a cemetery awaiting anyone who tries to bite off the corner and fails.

Following the climb out of the quarry to the fifth tee most will want to pause for a breather and admire the views over Wearside and Tyneside and out to the North Sea.

Only a strategically placed bunker prevents the fifth from being the easiest of birdie chances at 260 yards, but from this point the challenge becomes a little tougher.

The eighth is an attractive par five which sweeps sharply round to the right following a drive across a stream.

The second shot has to clear a rocky outcrop, which cuts off the view of the green, and while it is possible to

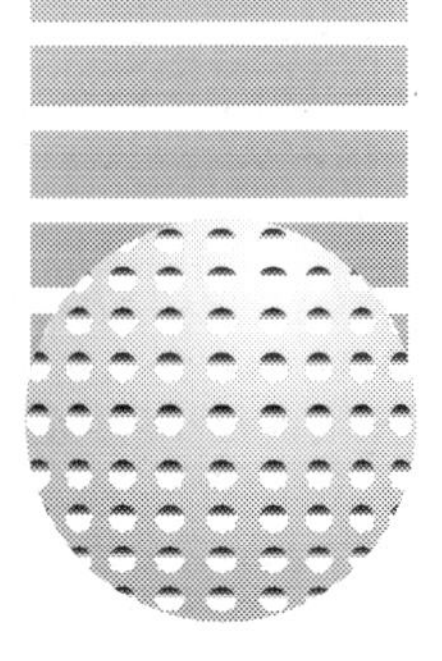

get home in two, it is wise to be wary of the out of bounds on the right.

Although the eighth is the shortest of the four par fives – the others are all over 500 yards – it is the stroke one hole.

Most, however, will find it more difficult to make par at the stroke two 14th, where the slightly uphill second to a well-defined green makes it play all of its 419 yards.

Out of bounds on the right and the narrow, sloping green add to the difficulties.

The 16th is one of the county's toughest par threes at 208 yards, while the 17th can be a very testing par four at 444 yards, depending on the wind.

The 18th is a par five with out of bounds again on the right and a hillock at driving distance on the left. At the foot of the hillock is a perfectly flat area no more than three yards square known as Dawson's plateau because it is reckoned that in his prime Dawson Hunter always used to land his drive there.

The club had an expensive failure a few years ago with attempts to build a pond at the corner of the dog-leg 13th. Otherwise their improvements, including extensive bunker and tree-planting programmes, have helped to enhance a very pleasant course.

FACTFILE

Boldon Golf Club Dipe Lane, Boldon, Tyne and Wear.

Telephone: Clubhouse (0191) 536 4182; professional (0191) 536 5835

Membership: 525 male, including juniors; 125 female.

Fees: £315, including VAT. Four-year waiting list.

Green fees: weekdays £16 (£10 with a member); weekends £20 (£12)

Course length: 6,338 yards, par 72.

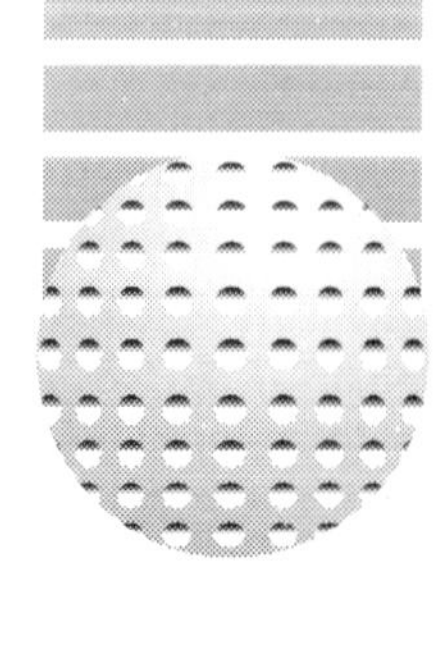

Tyneside Golf Club

FEW clubs have as rich a history as Tyneside Golf Club, situated at Western Falls, Ryton, just south of the River Tyne.

Believed to be one of the first 50 clubs in England, the original site was adjacent to the railway line on a 60-acre field known as The Willows, with the clubhouse a disused stick house dating from 1879.

The course was laid out by the club's first professional/greenkeeper Mungo Park, winner of the Open in 1874, who was approached when at Alnmouth, Northumberland.

Once the layout was completed in 1880 Mungo was joined by his nephew, the revered Willie Park Jnr, at the tender age of 16 and he remained there until 1890, during which time he won the 1887 and 1889 Opens.

Willie Jnr, who spent up to 12 hours a day practising his putting – believing that: 'The man who can putt is a match for anyone' – left Tyneside to work alongside his father in the ball and club-making firm of W Park and Sons before embarking on a career in course architecture.

He was accredited with more than 70 courses on both sides of the Atlantic before literally working himself to death in 1925. His courses include such masterpieces as Sunningdale and Carnoustie as well as local courses at Tynemouth and Hartlepool, and he also found time to write two books, The Game of Golf (1896) and The Art of Putting (1920).

Twelve years after Park's departure the Tyneside club negotiated a move to Western Falls, where they made do with a hotch-potch of holes until 1910 when Harry S Colt was commissioned to remodel the course.

The course has remained relatively unchanged from Colt's original layout. It presents a modest test at a par 70, 5,700 yards. But the subtlety of its undulating terrain makes it an intriguing challenge.

The 13th is definitely unlucky for some. It is the most potentially disastrous hole in the North-East. At 407 yards its length is its least demanding feature. Out of bounds lurks along its length to the left, while the fairway narrows at full driving range to a bottleneck. An iron is the choice of many players here, leaving an obscured view of the appropriately coffin-shaped green, which is cut into the bankside. Little wonder that double-figure scores are commonplace.

The key to good scoring at Tyneside is the ability to reach the seventh tee

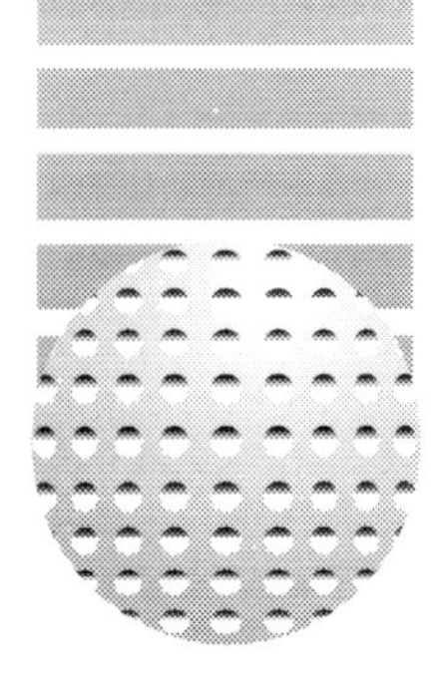

Tyneside Golf Club

Tyneside Golf course

mentally and numerically intact. The card begins with five par fours, the second providing the toughest challenge at 454 yards. A large pond bisects the fairway and can come into play for the big hitters or when wind is assisting.

The approach shot is played blind over a rise to a green which is perilously close to the out of bounds fence on the left. The eighth, played from an elevated tee, must be treated with caution, while the ninth is a classic short hole of 153 yards, where club selection is crucial. Anything missing the target leaves par recovery very difficult.

At the par five tenth a burn, which also plays a part in the next hole, must be negotiated from the elevated tee. The approach shot to the 11th presents a difficult challenge with the green situated tantalisingly close to a ravine.

The next three holes provide the course's Amen Corner where the faint heart hath no place. The view afforded from the 12th tee will take away any breath you may have left

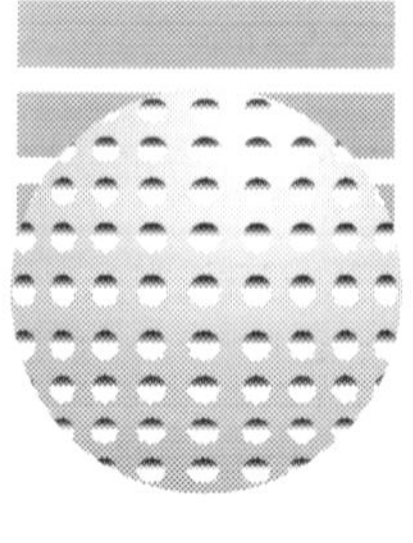

after the steep ascent to it, taking in almost the whole Tyne Valley.

The 14th appears ridiculous in relation to its sublime predecessor at just over 300 yards. However, the omnipresent out of bounds awaits the tweeker. Ryton church steeple provides the line on the last tee.

The professional, Mac Gunn, is by no means overshadowed by his predecessors, having competed in five Open championships in the company of the great Bobby Locke and Peter Alliss.

Mac, in his long association with the club, has played no small part in its ability to produce county champions and representatives in junior, men's and ladies' sections. There are more than 30 category one golfers at the club.

The clubhouse, an impressive wooden pavilion constructed by Alnwick Foundry, is a unique relic from the days of the move to Western Falls. Pride of place in the 19th goes to the club's magnificent trophy cabinet, a testament to the history of the club with the Thompson Medal (1880) and Reid Belt (1880) making superb centrepieces for the display.

A recent acquisition has been a series of frames of Willie Park Jnr in his heyday, which were taken from a film believed to be the first cinematic record of a golf match, between Park Jnr and Willie Fernie at Musselburgh.

The pleasant course is always excellently maintained, with the added attraction for the sentimentalists to indulge in thoughts of a bygone era.

FACTFILE

Address: Tyneside Golf Club, Westfield Lane, Ryton, Tyne and Wear.

Telephone: (0191) 413 2177

How to get there: Seven miles west of Newcastle on south side of Tyne on A695. Turn north at Ryton down to Old Ryton village, left past Cross Inn then right at end of row of old houses on right

SSS: 69

Green Fees: weekdays £22 day £18 for round; weekends £28 round

Course length: 6,042

Special deals: Reduced fees for parties of 24-plus.

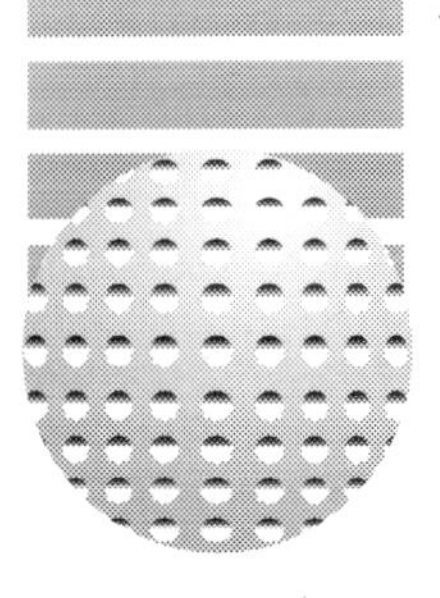

South Shields Golf Club

SOUTH Shields golf course, perched on the Cleadon Hills overlooking the mouth of the River Tyne, is one of the most consistently well turned out courses in the North of England.

The greens are renowned for their pace and trueness while the coarse grasses of the rough areas, if allowed to thrive, can transform the character of this sometimes benign test into a formidable challenge.

An excellent centenary booklet, produced for the 1993 celebrations, outlines the evolution of the club. It was produced by club member Mike Byrne and unearths a rich golfing heritage, such as the visit to South Shields of he famous golfing triumverate Harry Vardon, James Braid and J H Taylor, winners of 16 Open championships collectively.

Their two exhibition matches took place in 1905 and 1906 while another two all time greats, Abe Mitchell and George Duncan took part in a head to head in 1926.

The centenary committee's celebrations involved, among others, HRH Prince Andrew and Doug McClelland, former Dutch Open winner who played his formative golf at Shields.

One story which jovial Geordie Doug relates always raises a titter and is a reference to an occasion when Prince Andrew rang to arrange a coaching session. Doug's son answered the phone and politely enquired who was speaking. His Highness replied 'The Duke of York'. McClelland Jnr, aware of his old man's affinity to a tipple, shouted to him in the back of the shop: 'Dad, it's the pub on the phone.'

The course itself has a unique opening hole, a par three of 183 yards is a daunting prospect in itself while the boundary wall of the course runs the full length making this a hooker's nightmare.

The second signals a run of four par 4s of varying length, the 427-yard fourth being the pick of the crop with a scattering of fairway bunkers awaiting the stray tee-shot at driving length.

The fifth is another tough short hole at 187 yards with a well bunkered, coffin-shaped green difficult to hit with anything less than a top draw shot.

The boundary wall again plays an important role down the right of the sixth, a 512-yard par 5.

The tee shot is the key to muck or nettles with the abortive route left

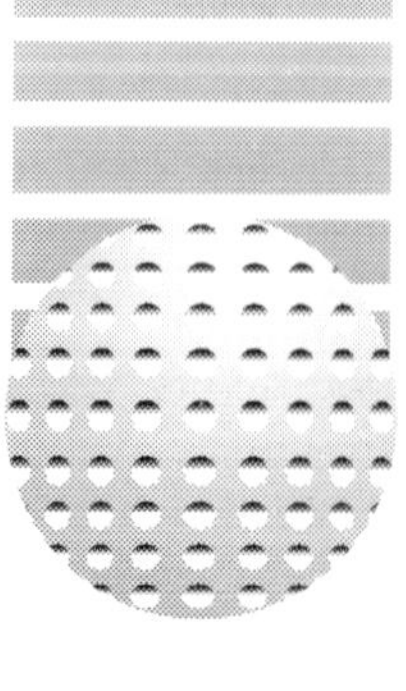

South Shields golf course

creating its own share of problems, a gathering bunker and very thick rough preventing an early escape.

The seventh at 437 yards played into the prevailing wind is one of the most difficult unbunkered holes in County Durham. The first two-thirds of the hole are played uphill, the tee-shot must bisect two grass hillocks either side of the fairway while a dry stone wall to the right adds its own hazard.

The eighth is a reachable par 5 at 470 yards, however, a tricky green is protected at the front by two large fairway bunkers making many a potential birdie turn sour.

The ninth and 11th are drive and flick par 4s, the latter, a slight dog-leg right, is protected by the omnipresent boundary wall the other side of which lies an old cemetery and has been the golfing death of many a good card.

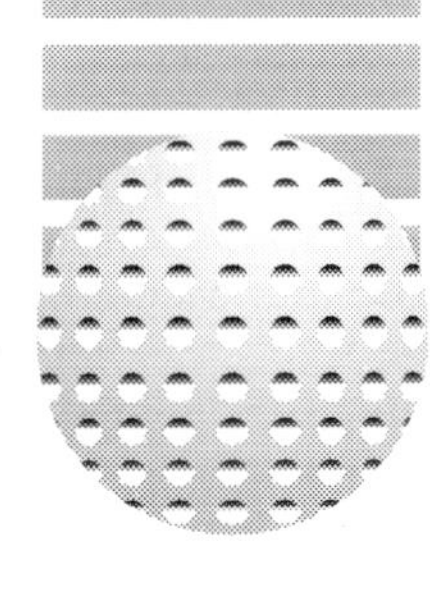

South Shields Golf Club

Sandwiched between these two is another good short hole at 179 yards while the par 5 12th offers a birdie opportunity provided strategically placed sand traps are avoided.

The 13th is the last and indeed, least complicated of the par 3s. Club selection error is the main obstacle on this hole which runs alongside the neighbouring course of Whitburn and signals the beginning of a notorious finishing stretch.

Five par 4s take you home, each with their own idiosyncracies. The 14th is the toughest at 459 yards uphill while the next two are within driving range for the big hitters as are the out of bounds and protective bunkers.

The penultimate hole is a genuine two-shotter at 387 yards, a severe slope left to right on the putting surface causes many an attack of the yips.

The 18th is a classic driving hole at 327 yards downhill, out of bounds awaiting the snapper, while the green nestles in the shadow of the club house.

The club has produced several County players of note. Bob Renaut, winner of the County championship in 1970 as well as numerous 36-hole scratch events, became one of that rare breed of golfers to achieve 50 caps for his county. The most famous amateur to have began his golf at South Shields was Dr William Tweddell, a surgeon who was to achieve national acclaim when he won the Amateur championship of 1927, following which he reached the final in 1935 only to be beaten by the lengendary Lawson Little on the final green.

Former Northern Masters winner David Conway has made several appearances for Durham while assistant Mac Joseph coninues to make inroads on the local PGA circuit.

An enjoyable day's golf is guaranteed on the Cleadon Hills.

FACTFILE

Address: South Shields Golf Club, Cleadon Hills, South Shields, Tyne and Wear.

Telephone: Clubhouse (0191) 456 0475; secretary (0191) 456 8942

Green Fees: weekdays £20; weekends £25

Course length: 6,264

SSS: 70

Other information: Special rates and catering facilities on request.

Washington Moat House Golf Club

Address: Washington Moat House Golf Club, Stone Cellar Road, District 12, Washington, Tyne and Wear.

Telephone: (0191) 417 2626

How to get there: Take the A194 exit from the A1(m). Watch for district 12 direction signs

Course: 18 holes, 6,604 yards

Special features: Parkland course. At the 6th there is a stream 30 yards short of the green. Treelined fairway

SSS: 72

Founded: 1979

Visitors: By appointment

Green fees: Weekdays £16; weekends £23

Special packages: Discounts and catering for groups available.

Further information: Nine hole pitch and putt, £4 per round. 24-bay floodlit driving field.

Crossing the stream at Washington

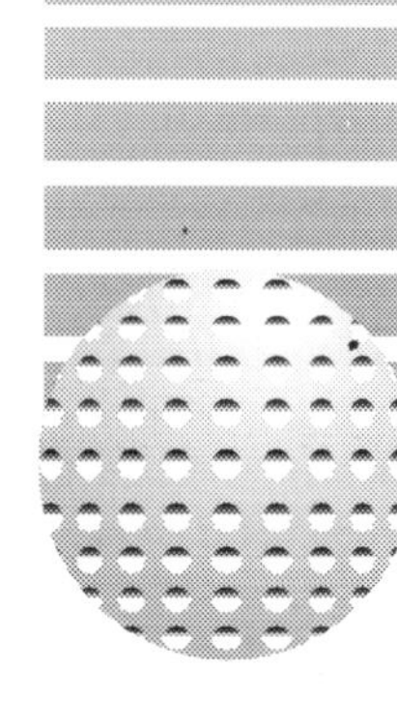

Roseberry Grange

Address: Roseberry Grange, Grange Villa, Chester-le-Street, Co. Durham DL2 3NF

Telephone: (0191) 3700660

How to get there: Club just off the Chester-le-Street/Beamish road and is signposted just before Beamish

Course: 18 holes, 5,892 yards

SSS: 68

Founded: 1987

Special features: Parkland course

Visitors: Welcome every day, but weekends often busy

Green fees: Weekdays £8.50, weekends £12

Special packages: There is a 17 bay golf range

Seaham

Address: Shrewsbury Street, Seaham, Co Durham, SR7 7RD

Telephone: (0191) 5812354

How to get there: The club is on the seafront

Course: 18 holes, 6,000 yards

SSS: 69

Special features: 13th is a par 3. The tee is built up and players have to hit the ball downwards among the trees

Visitors: Welcome at all times

Green fees: Weekdays £15, weekends £18

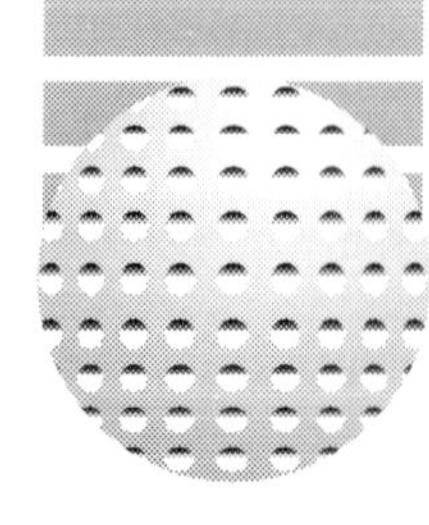

The 6th hole at Durham City Golf Club

The 14th green at Darlington Golf Club

The Chester-le-Street course with Lumley Castle in the background

The 10th green at Blackwell Golf Club, Darlington

Blackwell Grange Golf Club

The 11th, Blackwell Grange

BLACKWELL Grange is a fully paid-up member of the 'canny little course society' at just over 5,600 yards and with no fewer than seven par threes.

But the par of 68 is by no means a pushover and in recent years the club has produced seven players who have moved into the professional ranks.

The club was formed in 1931 on land provided by local auctioneer Stanley Robinson, who purchased the site when he acquired Blackwell Hall adjacent to the site of today's clubhouse.

The course had nine holes and shared facilities with tennis and badminton players and was similar to today's pay-as-you-pay public amenities. Clubs were available for hire and yearly ticket holders eventually became the nucleus of what is now the private members' club. The course was extended to 18 holes in 1971, when extra land was purchased.

The club has maintained a fun element to its golfing exploits over the years and with 250 social members on their books the 19th hole is guaranteed a healthy turnover.

The condition of the course continues to improve under the supervision of Neil Bursey and his four staff.

The par threes hold the key to scoring at Blackwell, the third being the only one under 160 yards. The fifth is an interesting hole at 164 yards,

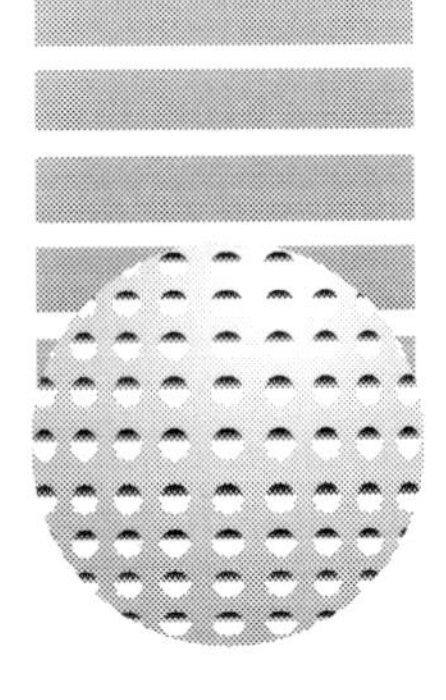

the elevated two-tiered green being well protected by bunkers.

The seventh is a reminder of one of the club's honorary members, Willie Whitelaw. The hole was named Whitelaw's Walk to commemorate his visit to the adjacent Blackwell Grange Hotel when he was Secretary of State for Northern Ireland.

Probably the best par three is the 176-yard 12th, which is also played to an elevated undulating green, which requires the utmost care and attention to avoid three or more putts.

The 14th is a demanding par three at 210 yards, while the 17th is a classic short hole played from an elevated tee to a raised, sloping putting surface. An unusual finish means the last hole is also a par three.

This provided an incredible finish to the club championship some years ago when Glynn Pickersgill holed in one to win the event by two strokes.

FACTFILE

Address: Briar Close, Darlington

Telephone: (01325) 464458

How to get there: One mile south of Darlington on A66, turn into Blackwell, club sign-posted

Course length: 5,621

Par: 68

Founded: 1930

Visitors: Welcome weekdays

Green fees: £20 per day weekdays, £20 per round weekends

It was a short par four until complaints from residents regarding stray golf balls meant the hole had to be reduced to 190 yards. The magnificent array of mature trees provides the main obstacle on most holes, not least the first, which is arguably the most difficult on the course. The second is also a superb hole, with the large trees coming into play and a strategically placed pond protecting the green to the right from the big hitters' attempts at reaching it in two. The 11th is an excellent hole with a wall of towering trees flanking each side of the fairway at driving length, while the 547-yard par five 13th is a test for golfers of all abilities.

Blackwell Grange is a unique club in many ways, their modesty being a rare attribute in these gung-ho days. A peaceful knock around a mild 18 holes in pleasant surroundings, followed by a pint or two in the snug pavilion – what could be more relaxing?

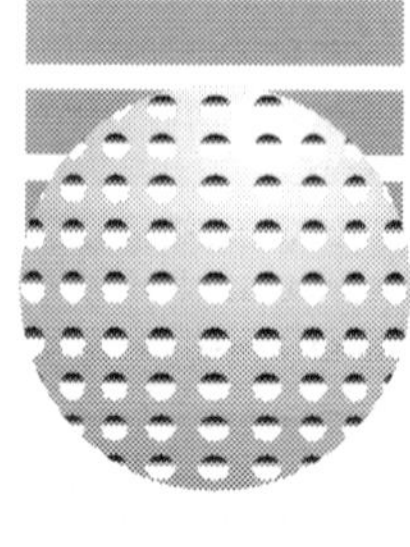

Ryhope Golf Club

Address: Off Leechmere Way, Hollycarrside, Ryhope, Sunderland.
Telephone: (0191) 523 7333

How to get there: Go through main street of Ryhope village until you come to old miners' welfare home on left. Turn left and left again at T junction. Go straight ahead and course is ahead of you.

Course: Yellow 4,486 yards, white 4,735 yards, 18 holes

SSS: 69

Founded: 1990 first 9 holes, 18 holes open since June, 1994.

Special features: Undulating combination of heathland. First 16th and 18th particularly good, 7 par three holes which are well bunkered and difficult. The last nine holes have had their greens developed and are excellent for pace and quality.

Visitors: Municipal course so open all the time, though weekends restricted because of competitions.

Green fees: Weekday £6; weekend £9 before noon, £7 after.

Further information: The golf course is very young but should mature into an excellent course. A new irrigation system is to be installed which should improve the quality of the course.

Aycliffe

Address: Aycliffe Sports and Leisure Complex, School Aycliffe Lane, Newton Aycliffe, DL5 6QZ

Telephone: (01325) 310820

How to get there: Take A68 from A1(m) then turn off for Aycliffe and follow signs

Course: 9 holes, 2,981 yards

Par: 68

Special features: Public parkland course. Driving range and sports and leisure complex

Green fees:

Weekdays £6, weekends £7. OAPs and juniors £4 and £5

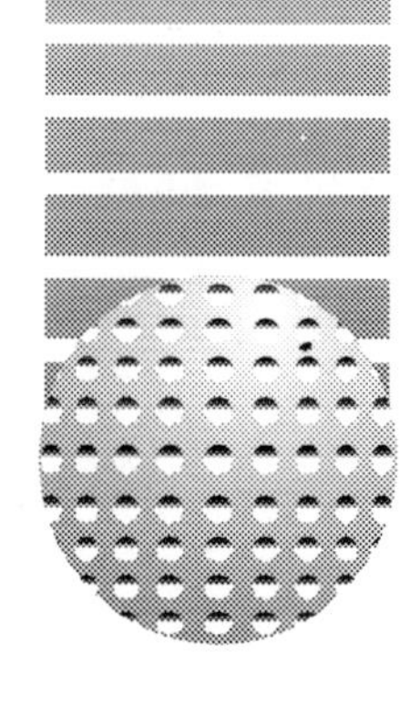

TEE OFF AT THE NORTH'S PREMIER MUNICIPAL GOLF COURSE !

Stressholme Golf Centre

The Golf Course is situated on the western outskirts of Darlington and is approached by the picturesque Snipe Lane. Built some 16 years ago the course and its facilities are now well established in the Golfing World and maintained to the highest standards. A view that is firmly endorsed by the P.G.A.
The Course istself extends over 145 acres and offers an 18 hole golf course of 5953 metres (6511 yards) Par 71, a putting green and practice area. Three car parks provide ample parking whatever the occasion.

- ★ **Superb 18 Hole Golf Course**
- ★ **Bookable tee off slots, telephone (0325) 461002 (casual slots also available**
- ★ **Available for visiting societies**
- ★ **Function Room available with Catering Facilities**
- ★ **New Floodlit Driving Range open**
- ★ **Resident Golf Professional**
- ★ **Practice area**

NEW!! DRIVING RANGE

Superb golfing facilities all year round!

Our prestigious new floodlit Golf Driving Range is now open at Stressholme Golf Centre, offering all-weather practice facilities. The range is situated adjacent to the first fairway and has 15 indoor and 10 outdoor bays (available in the summer). The indoor bays are fitted with 3 different types of matting to suit every standard of ability. The outdoor bays will enable golfers to practice in natural conditions. High quality practice balls will be provided. Visit Stressholme Golf Centre's new Driving Range for superb practice facilities, whatever the weather, all year round!.

Opening Times: Weekdays 9.00 a.m.-10.00 p.m.; Weekends 8.00 a.m.-9.00 p.m.

Prices: Small Bucket of Balls £2.00 (£1.75 Leisure Saver); Large Bucket of Balls £2.75 (£2.50 Leisure Saver)

For further details from the Golf Professional

Telephone (01325) 461002

A Leisure Facility provided by Darlington Borough Council

A Recently Re-Furbished 17th Century Coaching Inn

Situated 2 miles from the A1(M) and 2 miles from Woodham Golf Course with both Brancepeth and Darlington Golf Courses nearby.

All our 46 Bedrooms are en-suite with tea and coffee making facilities, and iron and ironing board, Satellite television, direct dial telephones, trouser press and hair dryer

Our Highwayman Restaurant with an excellent local reputation has a full a la carte and table d'hote Dinner Lunch and Dinner

A Conservatory Lounge Snack Menu available from 9 a.m. until 5 p.m.

Our Swallow Leisure Club is fully equipped with a heated indoor swimming pool, sauna, jacuzzi, steam room plunge pool and mini gym.

★★★

Ask about our Golfing Breakways which include Two Nights Accommodation, a Four Course Table d'Hote Dinner each evening, a Full English Breakfast each morning and a traditional Sunday Lunch or Table d'Hote on one day, Tickets for either Beamish or Bowes Museum and Whitworth Hall and Gardens and full use of our leisure facilities for ***£79.20 per person for two nights*** *(normally £99)*

★★★

Regular Dinner Dance and "Themed" Dinners included

Please contact our reception team for details on

(01388) 720451

GB5

CLEVELAND

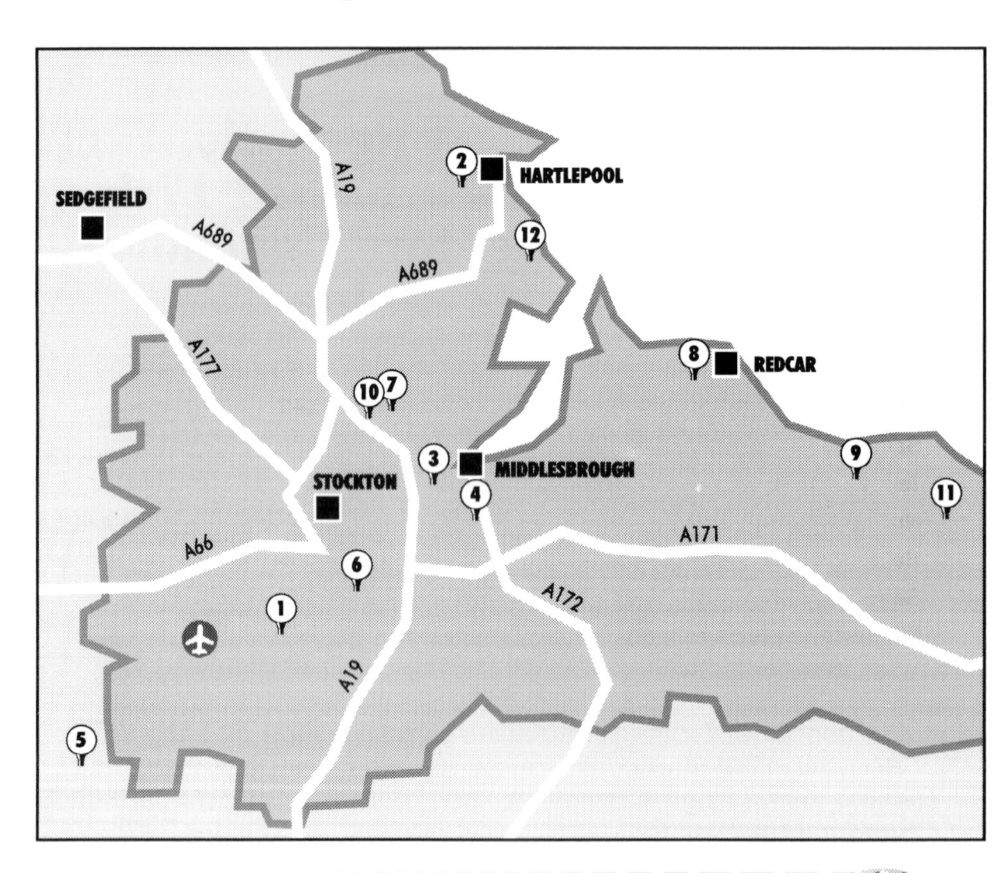

1 Eaglescliffe
2 Hartlepool
3 Middlesbrough, Brass Castle
4 Middlesbrough Municipal
5 Dinsdale Spa
6 Teesside GC, Thornaby
7 Billingham
8 Cleveland GC, Redcar
9 Saltburn
10 Norton GC, Stockton
11 Hunley Hall, Brotton
12 Seaton Carew

Cleveland courses

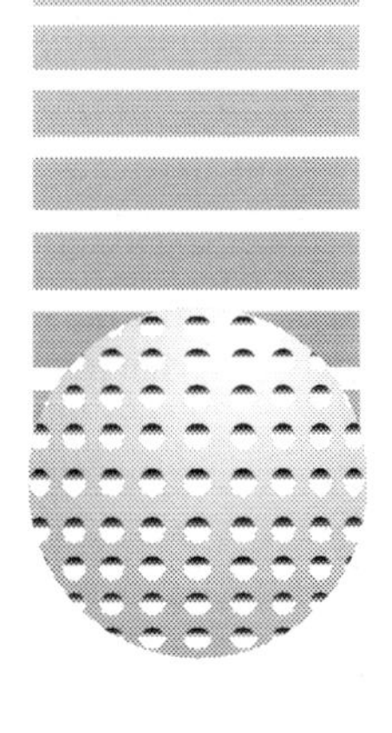

Eaglescliffe Golf Club

LONG-standing members of Eaglescliffe Golf Club have seen their clubhouse transformed in 20 years from the modest to the magnificent.

Until 1974 the club, which has spawned a long list of profesionals in recent years, housed its bar and changing facilities in two terraced houses on Yarm Road. Golfers had to negotiate the A135 on the way to the first tee and the temptation to throw oneself under a passing double-decker bus after a less than perfect round was all too inviting.

The clubhouse, built in 1974, gave special attention to making the most of the panoramic view from the lounge. The outline of the Cleveland Hills, including Roseberry Topping, provides an excellent backdrop to this interesting and varied parkland course.

With a swelling of the membership to 1,000, of whom over 200 are social members, it was increasingly apparent that further expansion was necessary. The club went about discovering what the members wanted in what, by golfing standards, was an unusually democratic fashion, drawing up a questionnaire which enabled them to identify clearly the top priorities.

Plans were drawn up by one of the members, a qualified architect, and the work, costing £300,000, was completed in June 1992 with an official opening by stalwart treasurer Jack Liddle in November of that year.

The club was founded in 1914 with a 13-hole course on Yarm Back Lane, moving to its current site in 1928. The course was designed by James Braid and with a par of 77 was one of the longest in the North of England.

But in 1939 seven holes were lost to the agricultural war effort and it was not until 1969 that extra land was purchased. Four holes designed by Henry Cotton were added, creating the foundations of the 6,275 yard par 72 course in play today.

Although the course contains a number of forgiving holes, its beauty lies in its ability to jump up and grab the golfer who dares to treat it with even a hint of contempt.

The 16th, a 467-yard par four, plays every inch of its length and requires a high degree of accuracy from both tee and fairway. The view from the 182-yard 17th tee is enough to worry even the most accomplished golfer. An elevated tee looks down on a two-tiered putting surface with a large pond and bunker protecting

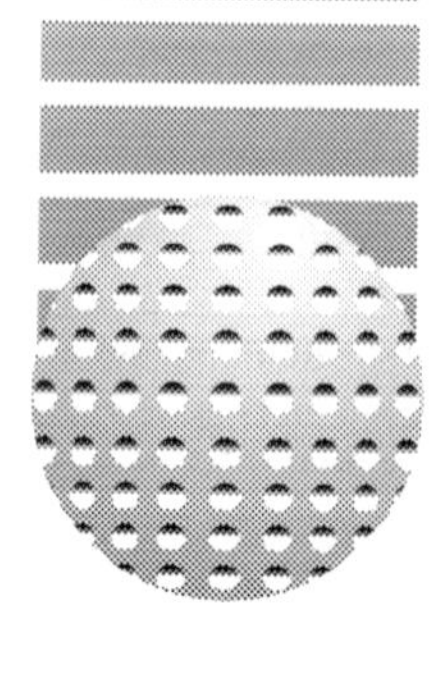

The river hole at Eaglescliffe

the front and right of the green. Club selection is paramount.

A similar degree of accuracy is required on the previous par three, the 200-yard 13th, again played from an elevated tee. With bunkers guarding the narrow basin green, players leaving this hole with a par consider it a bonus. The 14th, along with the 13th hole at Tyneside, is considered to be the greatest potential card-wrecker in the North-East.

From the medal tee the driver has to negotiate a carry of 150 yards over a slight bend in the River Tees to a fairway flanked by a tree-lined river-bank. The all-too-inviting bale-out route to the left is protected by a large mature tree and smaller ones beyond. The drive is by no means the

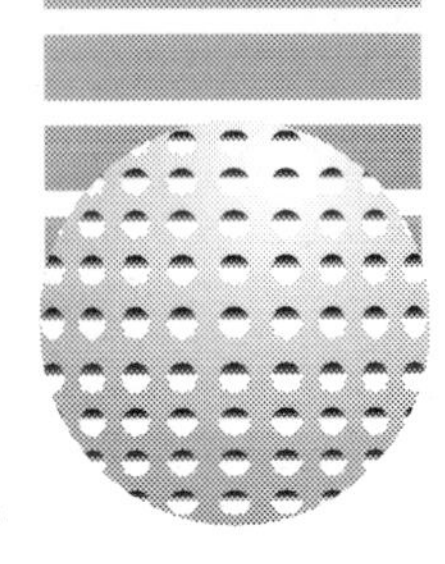

Eaglescliffe Golf Club

end to this 534-yard par five's perils.

The river runs along the entire length, and with copse down the left and three inviting fairway bunkers, as well as those surrounding the green, it is no wonder that scores in double figures, even in county championship events, are commonplace.

The 18th has all the characteristics of a scaled down version of the final hole at Augusta, and although measuring only 300 yards, out of bounds right and cleverly appointed bunkers make this a challenging end to the round.

An extraordinary number of Eaglescliffe products have gone on to join the professional ranks. Among them is Chris Davison, who after achieving success as a Durham County amateur moved to South Africa with his family in the mid-Eighties and has since won the South African Masters as well as making a significant impact on the SAPGA Circuit.

FACTFILE

Address: Eaglescliffe Golf Club, Yarm Road, Eaglescliffe, Stockton-on-Tees.

Telephone: (01642) 780238

How to get there: On left of A135 from Stockton-on-Tees to Yarm

Green Fees: Weekdays £22; weekends £28 (must ring to check availability)

Course length: 6,278

SSS: 70

Other information: Clubhouse recently extended.

Other pro's who began at Eaglescliffe include Robert Webster (Mount Oswald), Brian Rumney (Blyth) and brothers Steve and Paul Bradley (Billingham). Most of them owe a great deal to Jim Munro, who was club pro for 28 years until his retirement in 1991, a man who gave great encouragement to junior golf.

The husband and wife pairing of John and Lesley Still have contributed greatly to the club's county achievements, John having been Durham County captain from 1984-'86. Lesley, Durham Ladies champion four times, has also partnered Chris Hoggart and John Brown, himself a former NYSD champion, to the county mixed foursomes title.

The superb draught Bass and the excellent food provide the perfect climax to a visit to a club where, unfortunately for aspiring members, the waiting list is estimated to be ten years long.

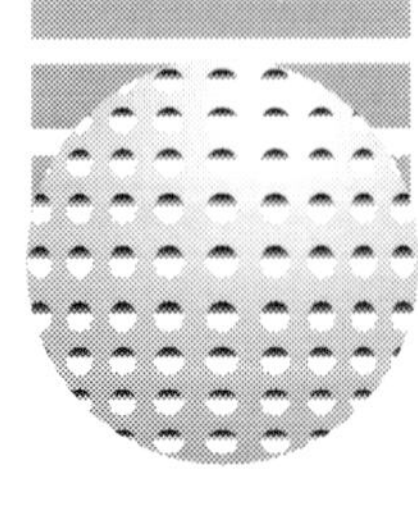

The 10th green at Dinsdale Spa Golf Club

The entrance to Hartlepool Golf Club

Hartlepool Golf Club

HARTLEPOOL Golf Club is strictly premier league. They have won an abundance of group and individual honours, while the course is ranked close behind its illustrious neighbour, Seaton Carew, as an intriguing linksland test.

The unique entrance is via a large housing estate, then through a tunnel under a grassed railway embankment, which completely conceals the course from suburbia.

The horseshoe-shaped archway frames the first inviting glimpse of the outstretched golfing hinterland on the other side of the track. To consider building a course on such rugged terrain must have taken considerable imagination, the club enlisting the talents of one of the greatest, many believe the doyen, of golf course architects, Willie Park Jnr, twice winner of the Open.

The club also turned to a legendary figure when altering the course in 1929. James Braid redesigned the tenth hole, an archetypal links par four where accuracy rather than length is the key to the drive.

The approach shot is then played over a ridge with the horizon as a backdrop to a green nestling among the dunes. The 11th, another Braid design, is one of four excellent par threes which many believe to be the key to good scoring at Hartlepool.

Measuring a daunting 223 yards, it is played across a deep sea inlet to a tricky putting surface, which slopes steeply from back to front. The seventh is at the other end of the par three spectrum at 122 yards.

But the tee shot is equally demanding, played from an elevated tee to a postage stamp green.

A marram-grassed hollow awaits the club selection ditherer. The 14th, the most difficult two-shotter on the course, carries the stroke one index and is played along a fairway shelf with out of bounds on the cliff edge left and a natural fall into rough on the right.

This hole has been the ruination of many cards. The 17th is the most recent to be rebuilt, this time by bespoke architect Donald Steel. One of only two par fives, it resembles more a parkland hole with fairway bunkers on the right at its dog-leg and out of bounds to the left.

The green has been intriguingly designed with two tiers and strategic bunkers. The course is very rarely closed, offering a red rag to the many golfing bulls who itch for a

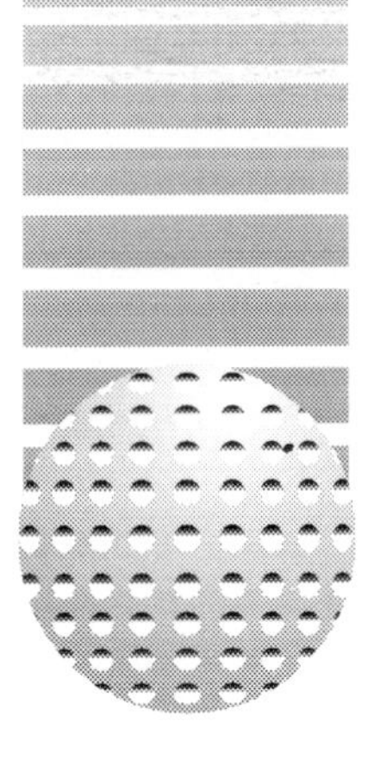

Hartlepool Golf Club

The 7th hole at Hartlepool

game in the winter months when their own pitches are sodden. And the club welcome visitors at all times. Four starting points are easily accessible from the centralised club-house, which is visible from every hole and stands as a classic Sixties brick emporium incorporating ample lounge and dining area, plus a snug containing a full-sized snooker table.

The club has produced an outstanding crop of club and county players over the years, the club's long-time professional Malcolm Cole playing no small part in their development.

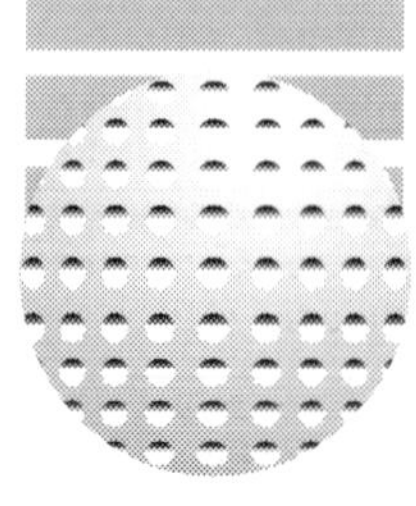

A tournament player himself, Cole has used the club's excellent practice facilities and his own no-nonsense techniques to give support and advice which has kept the club at the very top of competitive golf in the area for over 20 years.

Under the captaincy of Gavin Gordon the club enjoyed an unprecedented winning streak; recent honours including the Teesside Union A division title, Durham Teams Championship, Northumberland and Durham Dixon Trophy, Durham County Mixed Foursome and Durham Matchplay Championships.

While much of the club's inherent competitiveness must be attributed to Durham County champions John Wrigley (1965) and Alan Doxford (1975), the outstanding contribution made by Graeme Bell and county colleague Chris Marshall has catapulted the club to dizzy heights.

The bulldog spirit displayed by Bell, the 1989 county strokeplay champion and three times matchplay champion, has has had an infectious effect on his fellow team members.

One man in particular who has revelled in the club's success is former Durham County president George Olaman, himself a single figure player for countless years. Olaman and the late Harold Coyne, another ex-Durham president, were instrumental in much of the development of the club.

FACTFILE

Address: Hartlepool Golf Club, Hart Warren, Hartlepool.

Telephone: (01429) 274398

How to get there: Northern edge of Hartlepool off A1086

Green Fees: Weekdays £17; weekends £24 (not Sundays).

Course length: 6,255

SSS: 70

Special deals: Reduced rates for parties on sliding scale according to numbers.

The ladies have also produced a string of top-class players, the most notable being Christine Williamson (nee Barker), who represented England in the late Seventies as well as capturing numerous county and national honours.

Hartlepool is a role model of what many clubs aspire to be. The course is superbly maintained by head greenkeeper Alan Evans and his staff while the club's competitive and friendly atmosphere serves as a reminder that there is always a bright light at the end of the tunnel.

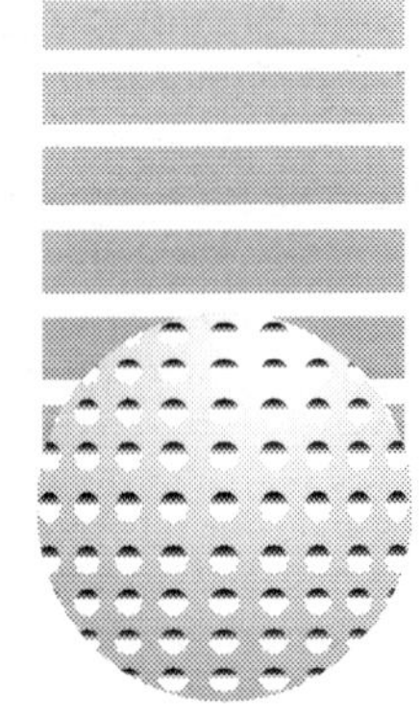

Middlesbrough Golf Club

THIS is the unofficial golfing capital of North Yorkshire. Situated in open countryside off Brass Castle Lane, the course was designed by the great James Braid in 1939.

The Braid layout remained relatively unchanged until recently when land was acquired beyond the original fifth hole and left of the eighth, enabling the greens committee, chaired by Stuart Hicks, to design three new holes and alter three others.

The new holes 13, 14 and 15 are cut into mature woodland and with rhododendrons and gorse enhancing their appeal they provide some of the finest inland holes in the area.

The major casualty of the re-design was the notorious par four 16th, which was flanked by a large ravine to the right and out of bounds to the left, with the landing area from the tee narrowing to 25 paces at around the 200-yard mark.

Many chose the soft option of two seven irons for safety, but among those who attempted to go for the green in one was Haydn Selby-Green in the final round of the club's North of England Youths Championship in 1979.

Despite reaching the 16th tee under par, he found himself several shots adrift of playing partner and eventual winner Roger Chapman.

The pairing had drawn a rather sizeable crowd, which had scampered around the tee in anticipation and were not disappointed when 6ft 5in Green decided to opt for the muck-or-nettles approach.

He reached for his driver but blocked his shot into the ravine. The gallery, many of whom had suffered the same indignity on this hole, remained nervously silent, but for a cry of 'that's gorn' by the club's chairman, Brigadier Claude Featherweather.

The atmosphere could have been cut with a knife when Green, having pegged up his provisional ball, proceeded to hook it into the farm buildings 60 yards out of bounds and unflinchingly cried: 'That's gorn'.

Realising even his faintest chance of glory had vanished, the Doncaster lad pulled out a full tube of brand new Balatas, laid them on the tee and systematically hit them one by one into the far yonder, each time followed by a chorus from the gallery of 'that's gorn.'

New holes have certainly added their touch of magic to a well-maintained course. The 13th is an intimidating

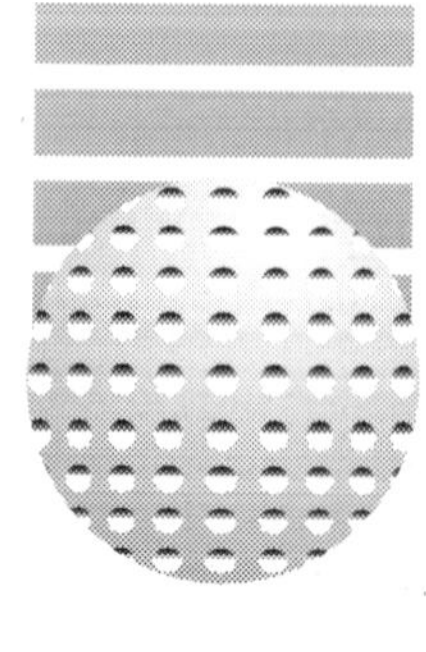

Middlesbrough Golf Course at Brass Castle

par four at 382 yards. From the raised tee trouble flanks each side of the fairway, which is crossed by a stream which comes into play for the longer hitters. Two large trees and a huge bunker protect the putting surface for the approach shot.

The 14th, slightly longer at 406 yards, demands another accurate tee shot with a fairway sloping to the right. The temptation is to cut off more than you can chew down the right, there being more room up the left than first appears.

The second shot is also difficult to judge as the green nestles in an amphitheatre of trees. The 15th is a tough par three at 171 yards over a small valley with a pond in the bottom waiting to catch anything which falls short.

The club has produced an abundance of talented players, the most notable being Martin Thompson, who won the Amateur Championship at Deal in 1982.

The man who played a leading role in the design of the new holes was

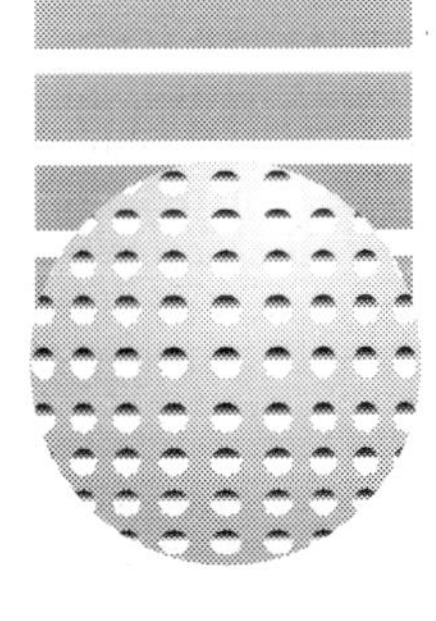

former county squash and hockey player Stuart Hicks, who is renowned in the Teesside area as one of the fiercest opponents in matchplay.

He still maintains a category one handicap, despite being eligible for seniors events, and although he was never capped by Yorkshire at golf, he has represented the Teesside Union more than 100 times.

The course is in very capable hands under head greenkeeper George Malcolm and his staff. George has been at Middlesbrough for 30 years and is a former chairman of the British Greenkeepers' Association. Club professional Don Jones combines his shop and teaching duties with often successful sorties on to the local pro-am circuit. He has made the bold step of employing a female assistant, Lawrie Rochester.

Andrew Nicholson, a former Yorkshire player, is attached to the club as tournament professional. Jones replaced Ernie Scott, a wonderful ambassador who spent over 30 years serving the club. He retired in 1986 and still makes occasional visits to the club, specifically on the day of the Colin Scott Open, an event played in memory of his son, who died from leukaemia when in his golfing prime.

Brass Castle is a fair test of golf, while not being too physical, and is invariably in good condition and well worth a visit. If you happen to bump into the infamous Selby Green on your travels and he mentions the 16th hole, you can say with all sincerity that it has well and truly gorn!

FACTFILE

Address: Middlesbrough Golf Club, Brass Castle Lane, Marton, Middlesbrough, Cleveland.

Telephone: (01642) 311515

How to get there: Five miles south of Middlesbrough, one mile west of A172

SSS: 69

Course length: 6,167

Green Fees: Visitors welcome on Weds, Thurs Fri; weekdays £26; weekends £32

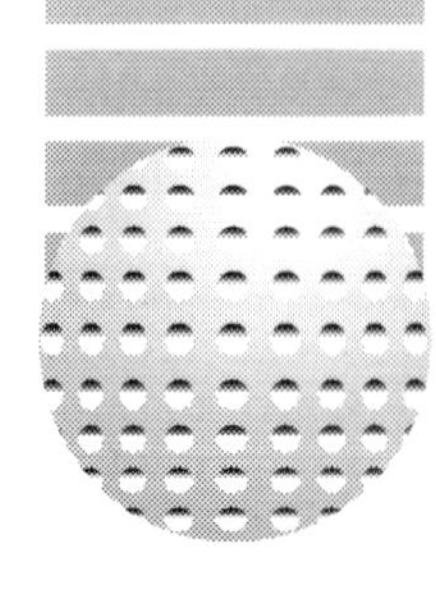

Dinsdale Spa Golf Club

THE tranquility of Dinsdale Spa Golf Course, situated on the plains of the River Tees with views of Roseberry Topping and the Cleveland Hills, is disturbed only by the occasional aircraft circling the nearby airport.

At 6,090 yards the course is one of least physically demanding in the North-East and relies on its abundance of bunkers and strategically-placed copse as its main form of defence, although out of bounds is never far away.

Golf has been played on the outskirts of the village of Middleton St George since 1902 with the current layout being adopted 20 years later.

The course is unusual in that the opening three holes are arguably the toughest. The first is a tricky 476-yard par five with ample landing area from the tee. It is, however, the green which provides its share of thrills and spills and is divided front and back by a tier 15 feet deep.

The second, a long par three at 211 yards, leaves little margin for error while most are still struggling to find their rhythm, a problem which manifests itself also at the third, a monster at 453 yards. The tricky green adds insult to injury before a retreat to the relative sanctuary of the fourth tee.

The next two holes are in the drive-and-flick category, while the sixth ranks alongside some of the best short holes in the area.

Played from an elevated tee, it is difficult to judge distance as the green nestles in an amphitheatre of bushes and trees while a brook and bunkers at the front await the club selection ditherer. The tee shot at the seventh tests the nerve with trouble on either side of the fairway while the undulating green at the eighth guarantees more of a challenge than its 133 yards suggests. Another mild par four rounds off the half.

The par-five 10th has recently been altered, making it the signature hole of the course. Originally a par four, the green has been moved back 70 yards the other side of a mini lake which acts as a magnet for approach shots, irrespective of distance.

The 11th demands accuracy off the tee with out of bounds down the left, grass bunkers and the inevitable conifers protecting the easy option right.

The 12th and 14th provide the two ends of the scale of par four status. The 14th needs two of the best to reach in regulation while its par four

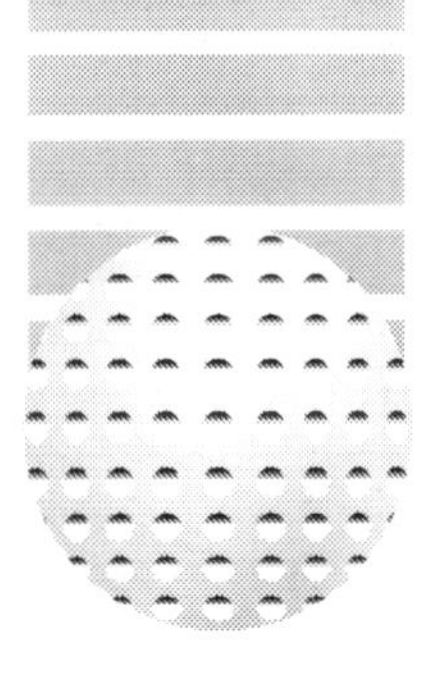

Dinsdale Spa Golf Club

Time to reflect at Dinsdale Spa

predecessor provides a glowing birdie opportunity.

Sandwiched between these two is a well bunkered par three while the finish leaves little margin for error. All par fours, the 17th is the cream of the crop where out of bounds and cannily placed pines add more than a hint of spice.

The course is in the good and, indeed, massive hands of award-winning course manager Tony Mears and his staff. A gentle giant at six feet five, Tony has been at the helm for around a decade after serving his apprenticeship under Roger Shaw at Billingham. His selection as 1993 Northern Greenkeeper of the Year has acted as a springboard to his lecturing skills.

Dinsdale's most distinguished player of recent years has been Ian Liddle, winner of the club championship on seven occasions. Ian even popped down the road and rattled off back-to-back victories at neighbouring Darlington in the mid-Eighties for good measure.

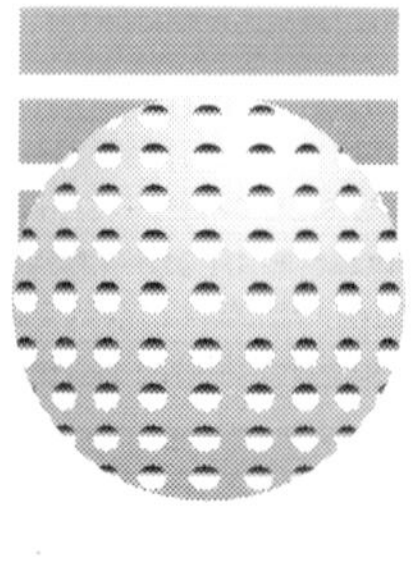

A scratch golfer for over a decade, Ian is a staunch member of the Teesside Union team as well as gaining his County colours and has rarely been out of the frame in the County championship.

Team manager Albert Goldsborough is another of the club's characters. His achievement of beating his age, off scratch, is one that only a handful of players can boast.

The ladies' section has always played an important role at Dinsdale. Kathy Bowerbank and Aileen Carter have achieved success in County events for many years and have inspired younger players such as Debbie Whalley, who has won the club championship on six occasions.

Dinsdale maintain a healthy junior section with brothers Richard and Stephen Musty, Malcolm Rose and previously Peter Ward and David Steele making their mark.

FACTFILE

Address: Dinsdale Spa Golf Club, Middleton St George, Darlington, Co Durham.

Telephone: (01325) 332297

Green Fees: Weekdays only (Tuesday – ladies day) £16 round and £20 day.

Course length: 6,090

SSS: 69

Special deals: Large practice area available (members only).

Victory in the 1990 Clark Cup was achieved by a pool of players under 30, the exception being Don Robinson, one of the best amateurs never to have represented his county.

The club house, built in 1965, benefits from its two-tier construction which provides an excellent vantage point for the course and its scenic backdrop.

Alec and Val Pocock, who have been associated with the club for several years, provide a varied selection of meals throughout the day.

The Dinsdale course is far from the most demanding in the area, yet it is always well prepared and gentle on the legs. However, as the club emblem depicts George slaying the dragon, one should never under-estimate the green beastie.

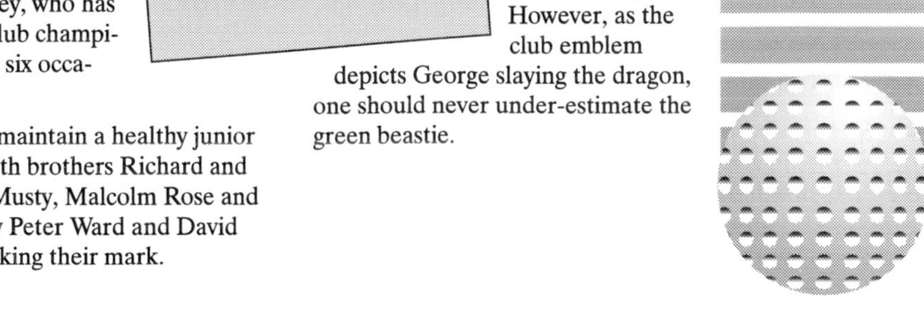

Billingham Golf Club

BILLINGHAM Golf Club stands as a monument to the vision of a group of local enthusiasts who turned a dream into reality against all the odds.

The course, a pleasant parkland test at 6,460 yards par 73, is situated on the outskirts of the industrial sprawl and has become a popular venue for both Teesside Union and Durham County fixtures, a great credit to the unstinting work over his 20-year association with the club of head greenkeeper Harry Lees.

The club has produced a booklet entitled A Phenomenon, outlining the origins of arguably the first municipally-funded club in post-war Britain.

This outlines how the club was formed, without course or clubhouse, in 1967 to pursue a project of acquiring an 18-hole layout. Political wranglings led to a document being signed leasing the area, formerly Northfield Farm, from the Billingham Urban District Council – less than three hours before the authority was disbanded to be replaced by the Teesside County Borough Council, which had threatened to oppose the deal.

The course was designed by Frank Pennink and uses the rolling terrain to good effect and with continual upgrading of teeing areas and the planting of thousands of trees in recent years the appeal, not to mention the degree of difficulty of the course, has been enhanced.

The first hole is a gentle 326 yards. However, the out-of-bounds fence guarantees more than a few anxious moments for the hooker.

At the second, a 506-yard par five, the green is protected by an all-too-inviting burn at its front while out-of-bounds lurks in wait to the left and back.

The third is a drive and flick while the next is a tough two-shotter at 416 yards to a green which to all but the awesome hitters is played blind.

The seventh has the boundary fence left along its full length and is remembered by many members and visitors alike for the previous owner of an adjacent field, a rather eccentric Russian, Mr Skripka, who came to England after the war and farmed his acres by hand using only simple tools and bedecked in his native attire. The attempted retrieval of golf balls which strayed onto his land was, to say the least, treacherous.

The eighth is a classic par three at 162 yards while back-to-back par

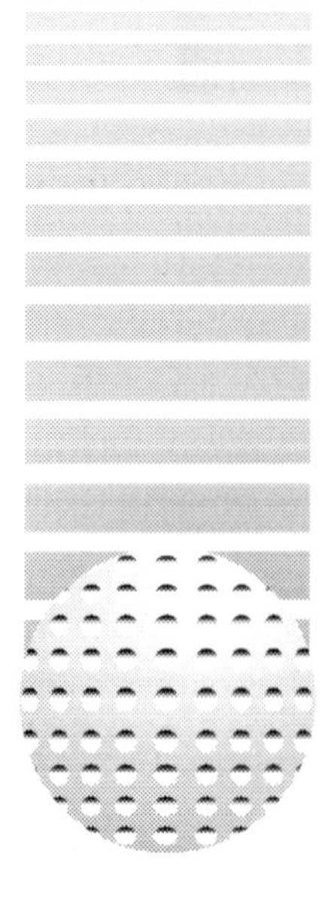

Billingham – probably the first municipally-funded club in post-war Britain.

fives provide birdie opportunities either side of the turn. The tenth invites the players to go for it in two, provided a large hill has been successfully negotiated from the tee. And a ditch crossing the fairway 80 yards short of the green awaits the mis-hit.

At the excellent 418-yard 11th, a water hazard runs the full length down the left and silver birches are strategically placed to the right.

The widening hazard, giving the effect of a dog leg, must then be negotiated in front of the putting surface on a hole which has proved to be many a golfer's Waterloo.

The trio of finishing holes are guaranteed to add spice to any game. The 16th is a well bunkered short hole played from a tee below the level of the green while the penultimate hole, invariably only a drive and pitch, has a steep descent to a large green leaving the judgement of distance irritatingly deceiving.

The last hole requires a good drive to overcome a deep gully while judgement of distance is again crucial for the approach shot to a green which is overlooked by the upstairs clubhouse balcony providing more than its fair share of drama.

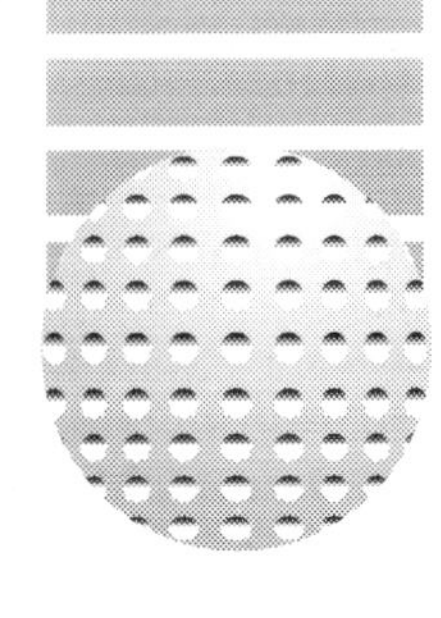

Billingham Golf Club

To have provided so many players who have figured consistently in local and national events in such a relatively brief biography is highly commendable and the competitiveness on which the club has thrived from its outset has been attributed in no small part to one man, the late Ken Walton.

His will to win on the golf course was legendary and proved infectious not only to his contemporaries, but also to the club's thriving junior section of the mid-Eighties.

In recognition of his achievements the club instigated an open 36-hole scratch event bearing his name which is also kept in the forefront of players' minds by his son Nick, who after an illustrious amateur career continues to make significant inroads into the local professional circuit.

Nick's partner in many club and county sorties, Mike Ure, is one of several Billingham 'bombers' currently pursuing a career in the paid ranks. He was North Region PGA rookie of the year in 1990.

The club has also produced a number of talented greenkeepers over the years. Roger Shaw, former assistant greenkeeper at Billingham, is one of the most respected head men in the North-East while Anthony Mears is course manager at Dinsdale and Paul Kellett continues to improve the course at Harper's on the other side of town.

FACTFILE

Address: Billingham Golf Club, Sandy Lane, Billingham, Cleveland.

Telephone: (01642) 554494

How to get there: Near town centre, east of A19 Billingham by-pass

Green Fees: Weekdays £20; weekends £33

Course length: 6,334

Par: 73

Special deals: Party concessions by individual arrangement with club.

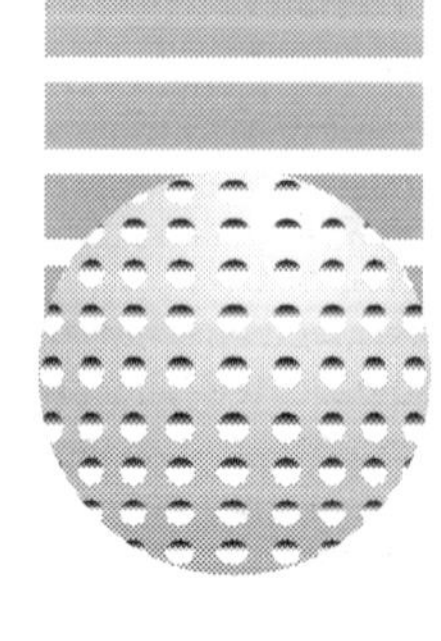

Cleveland Golf Club

THE drought which in 1992 became a major threat to Cleveland Golf Club was only the latest in a long list of obstacles which have been overcome during the club's long and illustrious history.

The only links course in Yorkshire has survived floods, the ravages of two world wars, sand extraction and the intrusion of a large steel works.

It continues to flourish and remains highly ranked in Yorkshire circles, just as it has been since it was founded on Coatham links at Redcar in 1887. It may sound slightly Irish to say that Cleveland is Yorkshire's oldest golf club.

But county golf does not acknowledge local government boundary tinkering and Yorkshire remain keen to use the Redcar course as one of their venues for top events.

The club is steeped in history and the centenary book, written by former lady captain Beryl Morris, records that the course was the brainchild of a Capt W Williams, Head of Coastguards. He had been stationed at Alnmouth, where a golf course already existed, and when he saw some people playing hockey at Coatham quickly persuaded them to try golf.

By 1890 the course had been extended from nine to 18 holes, and J W Taylor was appointed professional and greenkeeper. Taylor, who is credited with much of the work which laid the foundation of the links, set the course record of 73, which was equalled in 1896 by Open champion Harry Vardon.

The first clubhouse was built in 1891 and by the turn of the century Cleveland boasted a host of top county players, while in 1902 a ladies' section was also formed.

A matchplay event for the Calcutta Cup has been held since 1905, and in 1922 it produced an extraordinary climax when two of the club's most notable players contested the final. Cyril Roddam and Frank Robson had both won the cup before the war. And in their epic struggle of 1922 they came to the last hole then a par three all square. After Roddam put his tee-shot six feet from the pin Robson holed in one.

The Redcar course had to recover from the enormous damage inflicted during the Great War, when troops were drilled there. A nine-inch gun was placed on the 12th green and the clubhouse was burned down. It was not until 1934 that a new clubhouse was opened and six years later the links were again required for train-

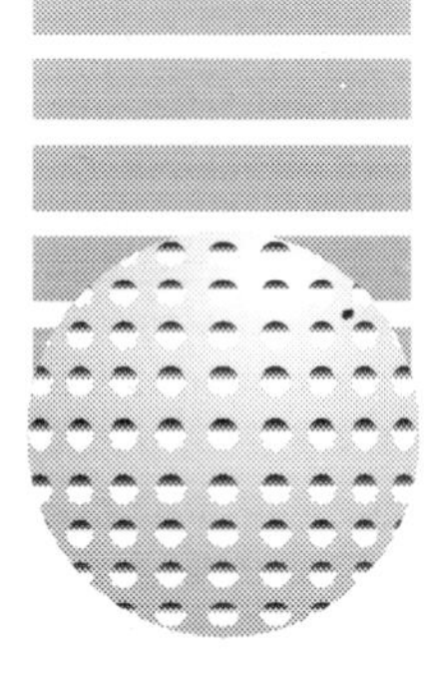

Cleveland Golf Club

Cleveland Golf Course at Redcar

ing troops, while mines were laid, along with an enormous tangle of barbed wire.

After the Second World War the club could not regain its pre-eminence in Yorkshire, although it continued to prosper at a local level. Most prominent at this time was Dr John Mackay, who became the first secretary of the Teesside Union in 1956, won its matchplay title ten years later and became its president in 1969.

Since then players such as Nigel Fick, Andy Gray and Heath Teschner, and more recently John Lines and Jason Jones, have kept the club among the trophies.

The Cleveland Salver, a 36-hole scratch event played in April began after a special tournament was held in 1968 to mark the opening of the revamped course over the layout which is still in use today.

The prevailing wind comes from the far end of the course, which has merely added to the intrusion caused by the steelworks. As well as bemoaning the ugliness of this blot on the landscape, golfers must also have wondered what it was doing for

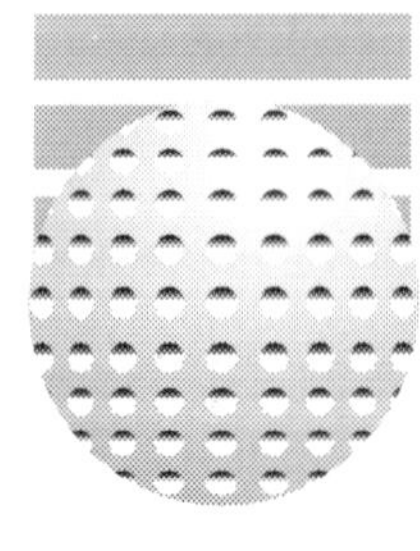

their health when the red ore dust was blowing across the course.

British Steel has taken steps to cut these emissions, with very pleasing results.

At 6,707 yards the course offers a good test even on the rare calm days and of the three holes over 500 yards, the longest is usually into the wind.

This is the 558-yard fifth, which can seem interminable if the ball isn't coming out of the middle of the club. It's a tough start, with the first measuring 372 yards to a plateau green which is difficult to hit.

The second is an excellent par three, the third measures 504 yards, and the fourth, a 415-yard par four, is the stroke one hole. Once past the fifth it becomes a little gentler through a series of holes at the far end of the course.

FACTFILE

Address: Cleveland Golf Club, Queen Street, Redcar, Cleveland.

Telephone: (01642) 483693

How to get there: Take A1042 to Coatham from A174

Green Fees: Weekdays £18 (members £9); weekends £27 (£9)

Course length: 6,707

SSS: 72

Special deals: Catering deals and concessions including evening meal and two rounds of golf for £28.

The 15th is an excellent par four set among the dunes, while the 17th is a magnificent 512-yard par five cut through humps and hollows, the largest of which makes the green invisible until you're almost upon it.

The 18th, a good finishing hole at 404 yards, is spoilt by the caravan site which separates it from the beach.

But the overall impression is of a course where it's good to be alive, where there's always a lively buzz in the busy clubhouse.

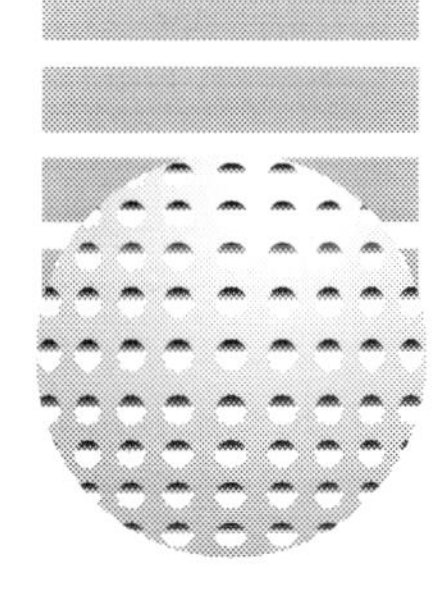

Saltburn Golf Club

THE view from the top of the sixth fairway at Saltburn Golf Club is quite breathtaking. The panorama extends beyond Roseberry Topping in the West, the foothills of Durham in the North and affords an uninterrupted view of the coastline to the East.

Very little has changed from the scene which confronted the visionaries of the course 100 years ago when a group of locals chose the Hob Hill site as their adopted home, having abandoned their original ground at Windy Hill Farm.

These dedicated golfing ancestors were very much in the minds of the members who attended the club's centenary year celebrations.

The task of collating the club's history fell unwittingly upon former ladies' captain, Sheila Atherton, whose original commitment extended to writing to the Royal and Ancient to settle a bet regarding the registration date of the Saltburn club.

That was duly confirmed as July 27, 1894 but the task snowballed into the centre-piece of the celebration; an excellent 70-page book chronicling the club's evolution.

Centenary captain Joe Baggot, the club's president and also captain in 1984 led festivites which included a match against Bishop Auckland and Bedale, who were both established in the same year and a fixture at Starbeck GC, Harrogate, who played their first competitive match against Saltburn in 1896.

The seaside course of under 6,000 yards flatters to deceive in the first five holes with three par fours of under 300-yards. These must be covered in near par to give the player any chance of a winning score.

The sixth and seventh holes do their best to grab shots back while the ninth is one of the best par threes in the area. At 166 yards the shelf green has an unforgiving fall to the front and left and is banked to the right with a bunker gathering more than its share of tee shots.

The tenth and 11th afford a slight respite while the 12th, at 223 yards, has capacity to wreck even the best cards.

The last six holes appear quite timid on paper, with two par fives included but any member will tell you that

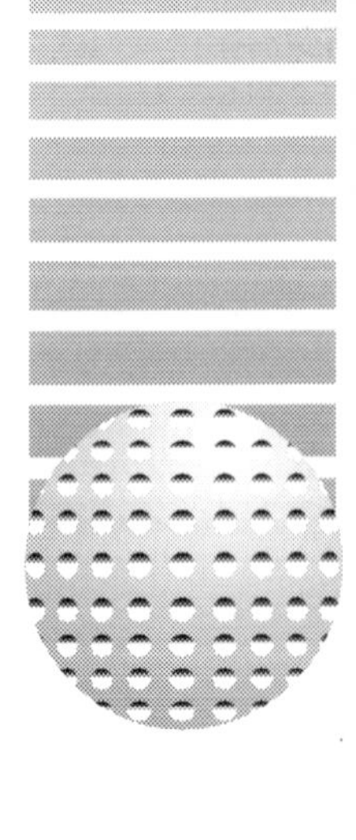

The golf course at Redcar

The 18th hole at Teesside Golf Club

The 16th green at Saltburn

they would accept playing to their handicap over this stretch.

The 18th hole is a magnificent finishing par 3 at 225 yards. Played from an elevated tee, the clubhouse entrance below is the ideal line.

However, the car park and out of bounds loom to the left and only the well insured should open their shoulders on this hole.

The club has produced some fine players over the years, including Harold Kemball, Teesside Union Matchplay champion and winner of his domestic championship on 13 occasions during the Fifties and Sixties.

Kevin Tucker, current captain of the Teesside Golf Union, has played a significant role for the club in competitive matches, his foursomes partnership with Nigel Fick giving the

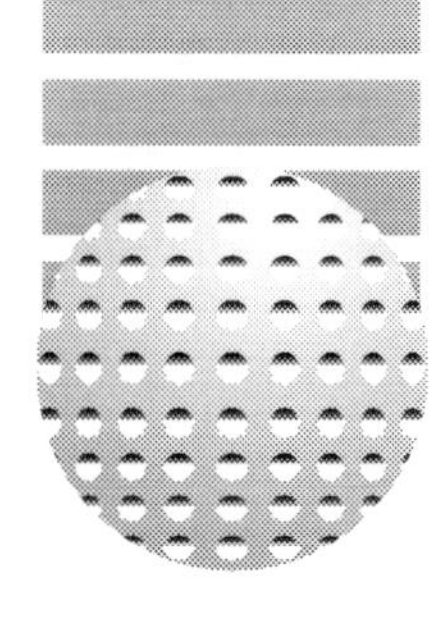

starters a few nervous moments when announcing surnames.

Kevin was rewarded by being chosen as the centenary year vice-captain.

Paul Benoliel and Jim McPherson have made significant contributions to the club's performances, while Alan Richardson, winner of the 1986 Teesside Union Matchplay, epitomises the Hob Hill definition – 'land of the mischievous spirit'.

Saltburn's most famous son, however, was Brian Waites, who was assistant pro for five years up to the summer of 1965. He went on to achieve Ryder Cup and World Cup honours as well as winning the Tournament Players championship in 1978.

The B team did their bit for centenary year, winning the TSGU B Division title after a gap of 11 years under the captaincy of Norman Hewitt.

The future looks bright for the club in the form of a 17-year-old Noel Emerson, who bears a striking resemblance on and off the course to Nick Faldo.

As for the authoress of the book, Sheila Atherton is a geographer turned historian and she has produced a superb read.

FACTFILE

Address: Saltburn Golf Club, Hob Hill, Saltburn, Cleveland.

Telephone: (01287) 622812

How to get there: One mile from Saltburn on A1268, Guisborough road on the left

Green Fees: Weekdays £19; weekends £22

Course length: 5,846

SSS: 68

Special deals: Special party deals by arrangement.

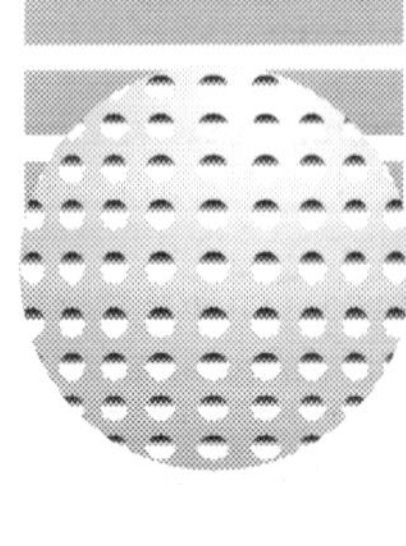

Teesside Golf Club

SITUATED just south of the Tees at Thornaby is the northernmost outpost of the Yorkshire Golf Union. But their contribution to competitive golf in a county which boasts more than 200 clubs has been very significant in recent years.

The club has had a chequered history since its inception in 1901, overcoming many hurdles, a by-product of its association with the ill-fated Stockton Racecourse.

This fighting spirit has spilled over into the club's achievements which include several Teesside A division titles.

The course has seen many changes because of the upheavals created by the battle scars of conflicting interests. However, with careful planning and unstinting hard work from former Cleveland head greenkeeper Tony Smith, who joined the club in 1980, the 6,500 yard layout is a well-maintained challenge to players of all abilities.

Strategy is very much the key to scoring on a course which can be separated into three segments of six holes. The first six are played on the most mature part of the course with tall, well established trees demanding a high degree of accuracy.

At the 360-yard first, the tee-shot leaves one acutely aware that wide is far from handsome. Driving off the second tee, the towering trees again give tremendous definition to this 539-yard par 5.

A drawn tee-shot for the right-hander is a must, while Thornaby cricket ground awaits anything pushed right for the second shot and a tightly-bunched copse to the left guards against the soft option.

Stories abound of cricket matches being disturbed by 'fores' rather than fours. The third is a dainty par three, while the fourth requires a well-placed tee-shot as the hole sweeps right. A fade from the big hitters will leave a short pitch, but out of bounds lays in wait in the form of a beck should you bite off too much.

The fifth, a par five at under 500 yards, is a potential birdie hole. Accuracy is again the key, while the sixth is one of the toughest on the course. The green, as with the fourth, is raised, making the possibility of getting up and down very difficult if the putting surface is not reached in regulation.

The seventh hole opens the second segment of the course. A tough par three at 190 yards, a par here is definitely a bonus.

Two mild par fours round off the half, while in contrast two par fives

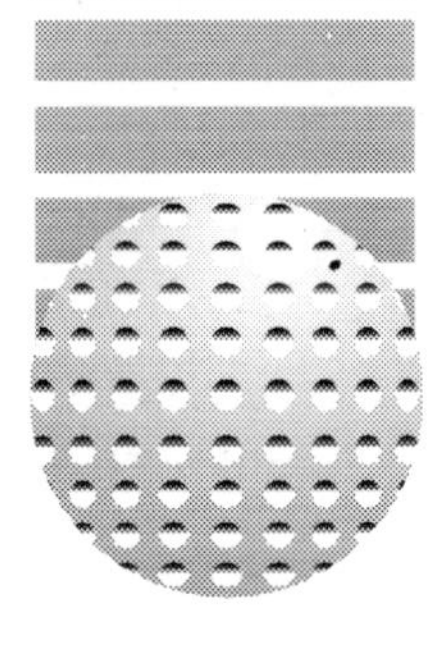

Teesside Golf Club

The clubhouse and bunker approaching the 18th green at Teesside

and a short four have the effect of lulling one into a sense of security on the back nine as they are followed by six of the best finishing holes in the area. There are three par fours over 400 yards, the first being the 433-yard 14th, a sweeping, dog-leg right with a bunker guarding the short route and an irritating ditch ready to catch the unwary. The 15th is a good par 3 at 163 yards, while the tree-lined 417-yard 16th sets a tough test. The 17th is a classic short par four where a crack at the green must be weighed up against tight out of bounds on the right and the over-hanging mature trees down the left. The 18th is another substantial two-shotter at 406 yards with what appears to be an ample fairway. But from an elevated tee, trouble looms either side, while club selection is

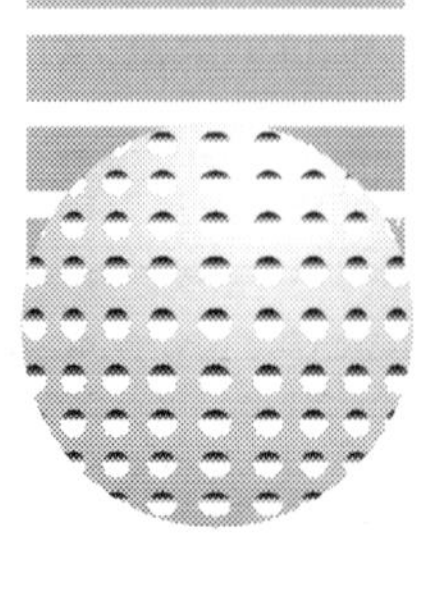

difficult for the approach shot to the green.

For golf even to be played at Teesside on the current site is testament to the unerring determination of a number of members, who just wouldn't give up when, in 1963, Stockton Race Fund, their landlords, threatened to cease racing and effectively evict the golfers despite having given them a 25-year lease the previous year.

There followed a long series of struggles and disputes until, in 1982, the racecourse went into liquidation. This initially threw the club into further turmoil but ultimately proved to be a blessing in disguise as it allowed the club to purchase the land from the liquidators and give them their first taste of stability for decades.

The club lost some of its better players during this period of uncertainty. But among those who remained were Tim Gifford, Wally Hill and Peter McCoach, making sure Teesside was kept on the local golfing map with victories in Teesside Union Strokeplay and Matchplay championships as well as elsewhere.

It is appropriate that the club should have played such a prominent role in the Teesside Union as it was in their clubhouse bar that the inaugural meeting was held.

Rarely have we been inundated with such co-operation and information when visiting a golf club and we can assure anyone who visits that they will be afforded the unadopted slogan of Teesside Golf Club that there is no such thing as strangers in golf, just friends they haven't yet met.

FACTFILE

Address: Teesside Golf Club, Acklam Road, Thornaby-on-Tees, Cleveland

Telephone: (01642) 676249

How to get there: Off A19, take A1130 to Stockton. Course one mile from A19 on the right

Green Fees: visitors up to 4.30pm, bookings by phone; weekdays £20 (£10 with adult member); weekends £26 (£13)

Course length: 6,515

SSS: 71

Special deals: Parties of ten or more qualify for discounts.

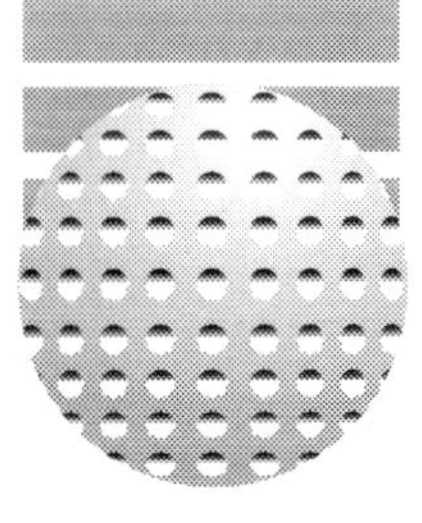

Norton Golf Club

THIS little-known course, adjoining Harpers Garden Centre at Norton, near Stockton-on-Tees, deserves greater recognition.

It features one of the most difficult holes in the region plus several other wonderful surprises since being extended to 18 holes in 1992.

The first is an attractive dog-leg skirting round two ponds, and the second is a delightful par three with a 90-yard carry over a lake created from a woodland bog.

But the fifth is the major talking point. Purists might argue that it's unfair and decide they'd rather tangle with an enraged pit bull terrier than risk the mental scars of a quadruple bogey.

But this is a course built for enjoyment and most golfers will relish the challenge of this extraordinary hole.

A 480-yard par five, it starts with a drive across a valley side, where a slice or an unkind bounce will throw the ball into the stream or bushes at the bottom.

Bunkers have been positioned to catch anyone taking the safe route up the left.

Assuming the drive lands safely, another good hit is needed up on to the level ground above, followed by a chip down to the green, set by the stream in the wooded valley.

The green becomes visible only when you get within 100 yards of it, and any big hitters trying to get home in two will find their approach blocked by trees.

The danger of overshooting the narrow green with the third shot means most will take the safer option of trying to run the ball down the steep bank. The fifth is one of three par fives on the 6,150-yard pay-as-you play course.

It lies behind Harpers Garden Centre on Junction Road, Norton, and is the latest extension of a family-run business which has other families very much in mind.

'Since we opened the nine-hole course it has given lots of people the chance to play who would not have thought of it before,' said Alan Harper.

His wife Margaret added: 'Husbands can have nine holes of golf while their wives go round the garden centre. Then they meet for a meal in the bar afterwards.'

Alan says: 'We have no great ambitions for the course. There's a big gap in the market for pay-as-you-play courses and we don't want to

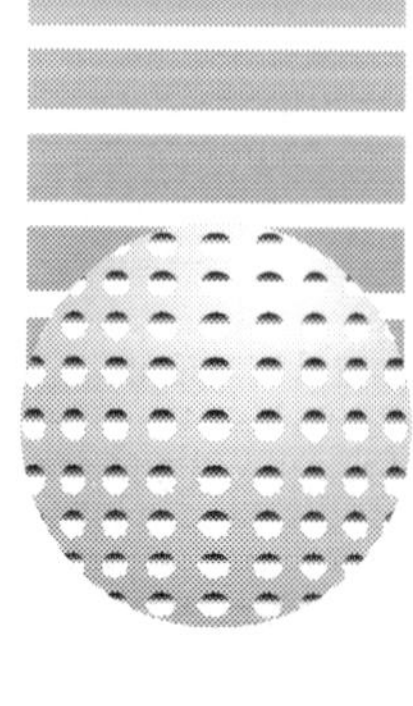

Norton – a course built for enjoyment

price it beyond the reach of working people.

'Learning their golf here has opened up something new for a lot of people. It has given them the confidence to go and play other courses.

'We insist on proper dress and we have three stewards who make sure the rules of golf are applied.

'Some players have formed a society and when they go elsewhere we often get good feedback about their behaviour.'

Alan is a landscape contractor who started work as a 15-year-old at Strikes Garden Centre at Eaglescliffe.

Even the family sheepdogs are involved. With no training, they have learned to find lost golf balls, even from the ponds, and by selling them at 50p a ball the Harpers have raised more than £1,000 for cancer relief.

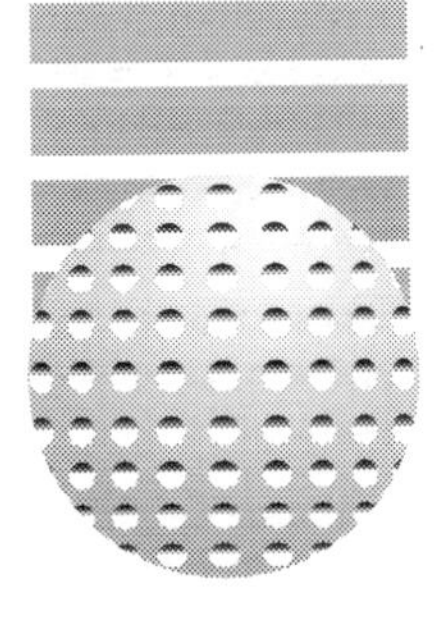

Norton Golf Club

Tim, who works with his father on the golf side of the business, drew the plans for the course and they did the landscaping together.

They have previous golf course experience at Wilton, Bedale and Brass Castle, and, working with an architect, they built Woodham from scratch.

With nearby courses such as Billingham and Eaglescliffe having five-year waiting lists, the Harpers moved quickly when a 70-acre farm became available behind their original course. They built 13 new holes and reduced the nine to five, making the holes longer.

The first two were combined to make a good par four opening hole, followed by a lengthy walk to the newly-acquired land.

The second, the par three over the lake, is a lovely hole by any standards, while the third climbs up on to open fields, leaving Teesside suburbia well behind and opening up panoramic views to Wynyard Hall and beyond.

Apart from shaping the greens and tees and digging out the well-shaped bunkers, little earth has been moved.

'Most designers seem to move everything,' said Alan. 'We kept earth moving to a minimum because it causes structural damage to the soil and interferes with drainage. A course can take a long time to recover from that.'

Alan believes the course would not be a successful business venture had they not been able to build it themselves. And he warns farmers thinking of converting their land into a golf course to be very wary.

But Alan admits now that he might even be tempted to take up the game himself!

FACTFILE

Address: Norton Golf Club

Junction road, Stockton-on-Tees, Cleveland TS20 1SU

Telephone: (01642) 676385

Course length: 5,855

Par: 70

Green fees: £8.50 per round, £13.50 per day weekdays, £9 per round, £15 per day weekends and Bank Holidays

Special packages: Societies welcome by arrangement

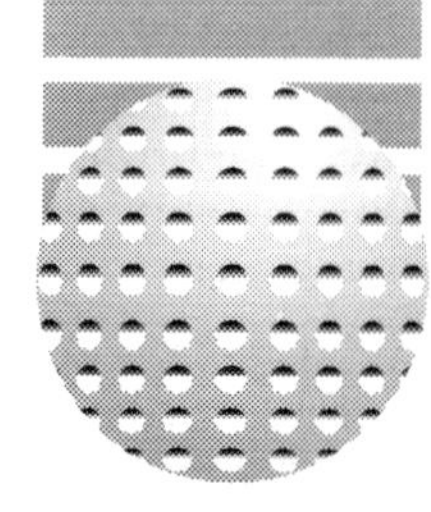

Hunley Hall Golf Club

A SLOPING tract of arable land may not sound like the most obvious site for a golf course.

Particularly when its access road starts among the allotments and pigeon crees which have long provided the traditional recreation of industrial East Cleveland.

But the Hunley Hall club, at Brotton, which opened in the summer of 1993, already has golfers flocking to its well-contoured fairways. The dramatic setting, with stunning views of Boulby cliffs, provides the course's biggest natural asset, which had been pointed out by golfing friends of farmer John Askew for many years. Otherwise the creation of a demanding and highly enjoyable test of golf from rape and barley fields has required quite a transformation.

Work began in March 1992, and in less than four months 60,000 cubic metres of earth were shifted on the 150-acre site. Four water features, mounds, hollows, and even a valley where previously a steep slope existed, were created as the 6,918-yard course took shape alongside the driving range.

A year after the contractors moved off site the course opened for play and Askew had himself a superb golf course for the bargain price of around £450,000.

He spent around the same on a luxurious two-storey clubhouse, which must be unique in boasting views of all 18 holes.

When Askew finally decided that stories about farmers turning to rape were old hat, and that his land really was suitable for golf, he played an early master stroke by enlisting the services of Bryan Moor, of OCM Associates.

Moor is the Scarborough-born, Scotland-based course architect behind several ventures in the North, including the nine-hole course at Hall Garth Hotel, near Darlington, and the re-design at Barnard Castle. 'I was involved virtually from the start,' he said.

'I knew straight away that the outstanding scenic beauty of the place would give the course a special charisma. The council planners wanted the clubhouse at the top of the hill near the allotments but I persuaded them it would be impossible to build the 18th hole up such a steep slope.

'When we had chosen the clubhouse site we looked out and John said all the land I could see was his.

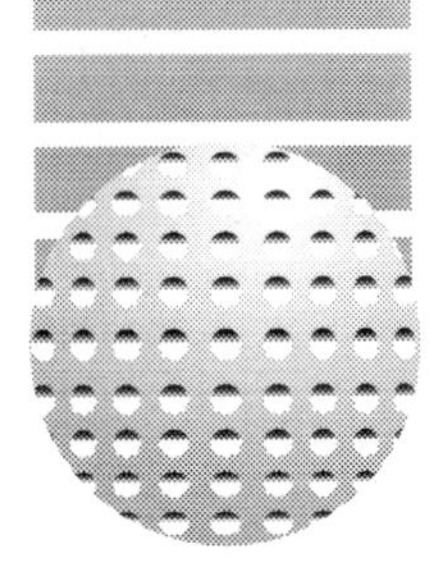

Hunley Hall Golf Club

Hunley Hall Golf Club, Brotton

'But when I submitted my first plans he said it looked fine, but most of the land I'd worked on did not belong to him!'

Knowing the planning hurdles which always crop up, Moor is used to doing several designs and the first plans they put forward were turned down because of National Trust objections. Heritage Coast restrictions meant they had to bring the course inland away from the cliff edge and the Cleveland Way.

They also planted gorse and 16,000 trees, which had to be of varieties which were natural to the area such as oak, ash, rowan, blackthorn, hawthorn and juniper among others.

'The National Trust man said we would never get trees to grow here, and he was standing in the shade of one at the time,' said Askew.

'People put every possible objection in your way, but now they have seen what we have created they seem very happy.

'I am not a golfer and when a friend suggested 18 years ago that I should build a golf course here I laughed at him. Finally we decided we wanted to be out of agriculture.

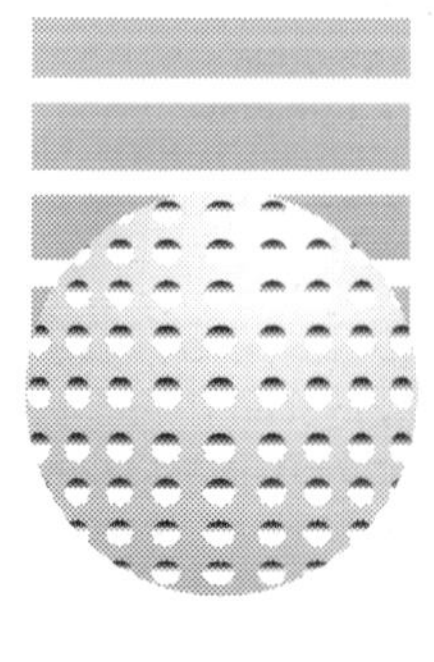

Hunley Hall Golf Club

'I totally disagreed with the policy of setting land aside. I wanted to see my land put to use, and now I'm delighted to see people enjoying themselves on it.

'If we had just wanted to make money we could have built a pay-as-you-play course. But we wanted to create something special and we hope to have tournaments played here. Most of our members used to play at Saltburn or Whitby, where they were used to wide open spaces.

'Here we have gorse and blackthorn to give the course definition and punish wayward shots. Reaction to it has been very encouraging. Everyone says it's challenging.'

Askew and his wife Ann had farmed at Hunley Hall for 30 years, and still have 200 acres, part of which might be used to build a further nine holes. Ann is now the company secretary and two of their four daughters also work at the club, along with son-in-law Andrew Lillie, who is the clubhouse manager.

'The farm used to provide work for six people, now there are 21 of us running the golf club, including green staff,' said Askew. 'We have bars upstairs and down, a large dining room and a dance floor. We have a full pub licence, so we're not catering just for members.

There's nowhere else between Redcar and Whitby which can cater for groups of 150. We're doing as well as we had hoped in the clubhouse and better than expected on the course.

Because they want to attract a lot of visiting parties, they have put a ceiling of 500 on membership.

The first captain was Alan Walker, who originally suggested the course 18 years ago...

FACTFILE

Address: Hunley Hall Golf Club, Brotton, Saltburn, Cleveland.

Telephone: (01287) 676216

Green Fees: weekdays £18; weekends £25

Course length: 6,918

SSS: 68

Special deals: Minimum 8 players, 27 holes, catering included from £26.

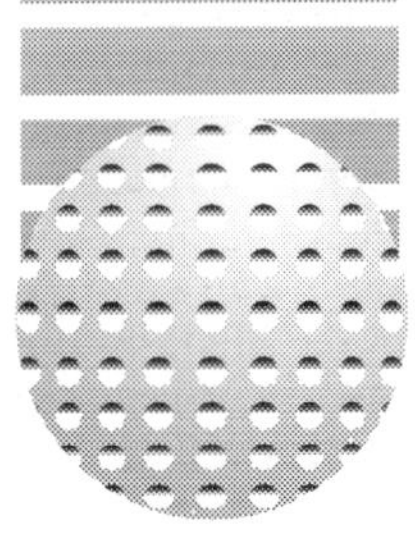

Seaton Carew Golf Club

Seaton Carew is considered by many as the jewel in the Crown of North-East golf courses. A true links, Seaton's backdrop is blighted by Teesside's heavy industry, therefore the course relies on its own special qualities for its reputation.

While Golf World magazine's list of the top 50 courses in the British Isles continues to show the North-East as a vast golfing desert, there are many who feel that Seaton, at least, should be included. First impressions are that the club is content to keep a low profile. Visitors driving along the seafront couid easily miss the unimposing entrance. The course also maintains a strong and silent dignity, having no need of modern gimmicks to present golfers of all abilities with an enjoyable test. Its beauty lies in the way in which it uses the wild, duneland terrain to optimum effect in presenting a challenging variety of holes. The third is a daunting 172-yard par three to an island green surrounded by steep-banked bunkers, while the 13th is an intimidating 537 yards, with a narrow fairway flanked by the all too inviting buckthorn. But the 17th commands the greatest number of expletives from its would-be conquerors. At 413 yards and with a generous landing area, the hole does not at first sight seem too difficult. However, the approach to the narrow pear-shaped triple-tiered green is fraught with danger and a visit to any of the four bunkers demands a skilful deftness of touch to extricate oneself and still remain on the putting surface. Stories of the 17th hole are revealed on the folklore of Seaton Carew, alongside such events as the playing of the course in the 1930s by HRH The Prince of Wales, later King Edward VIII. A photograph and autograph chronicling his visit are proudly displayed in the clubhouse, where the delights include the excellent value of the pickled eggs and jumbo sausages as well as more exotic fare.

Seaton has played host to a number of national events. As well as the Brabazon Trophy in 1985, won by Catterick's Roger Roper in a tie with Peter Baker, later to become Benson and Hedges international champion at Fulford, the club has twice hosted the British Boys Championship in 1978 and 1986. Established in 1874 as The Durham and Yorkshire Golf Club, Seaton is one of the oldest courses in Britain and one of the first 50 in the world. It is a true championship course and, along with its neighbour Hartlepool, is one of the very few links courses to be

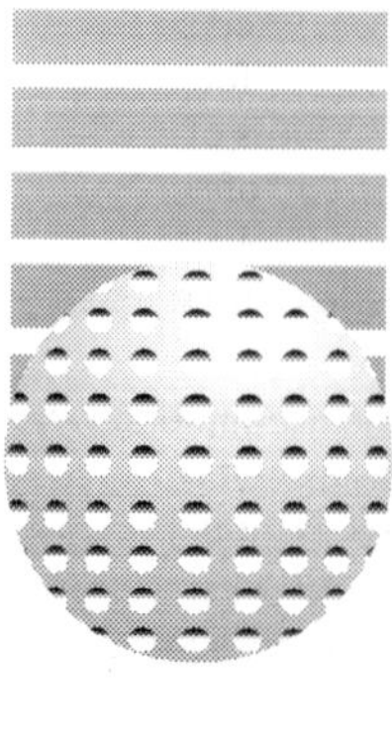

Seaton Carew Golf Club

Seaton Carew – A true links course

found on the East coast of England. Many improvements have been made to the lay-out, including the extension to over 6,500 yards in 1925 by the architect of the U.S. Masters course at Augusta, Dr Alister Mackenzie. But it was in the club's centenary year, 1974, that they embarked upon the creation of a loop of four holes, which now forms the basis of the Brabazon course, named after the English Amateur Strokeplay Championship which was held there in 1985.

It is as much the characters as the course which make Seaton special, not least the professional Bill Hector. Bill has been the club's pro for 30 years, having turned to the paid ranks after gaining a degree in agriculture and being awarded a golfing blue at Aberdeen University. Bill made the long journey south to Sunningdale, where he learned his trade as one of six assistants to the then guru of teaching professionals, Arthur Lees.

It was after his move to Colchester in 1961 that Bill gained a number of creditable finishes on the UK tour, and along with Brian Wilkes won the Martini International foursomes at The Berkshire – an achievement that was to give him a lifetime exemption from pre-qualifying. This is gratefully accepted now when, at 57, Bill has a new lease of life playing in the growing number of Seniors Tour

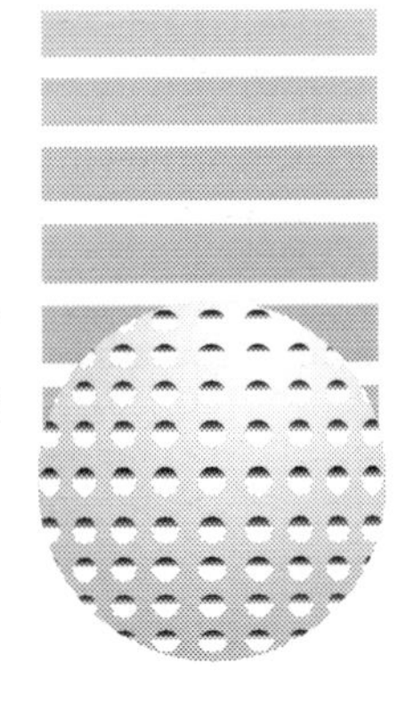

events. Although playing and competing are still his passion, Bill derives a great deal of pleasure from teaching and has been responsible for the achievements of Seaton's home-bred players such as David Whelan, Barcelona Open champion in 1988, double county champion John Ellwood, and England international and now PGA North Region tournament winner Alex Robertson.

Another popular character at the club is greenkeeper Peter Green, who reckons tricks of the trade learned through 40 years of experience are the secret of Seaton Carew's excellent greens. Peter, 57, has worked at the club since he was 17. 'People coming into the job these days all have pieces of paper to show that they know it all in theory,' he said. 'But you can't learn the job in a classroom.'

Seaton's greens are in superb condition all year round, but Peter says he has no particular secrets. The sandy soil means the course is never waterlogged, but he has been grateful for the recent wet summers.

Peter used to play to four handicap as a member of the artisans club which was attached to Seaton Carew. but now that the club has folded he rarely plays. 'I enjoy the work,' he said. 'We like to think it's the best course in the North-East, and I'll have clocked up nearly 50 years here when I retire.'

One of the most outstanding features of this demanding links course is the effect the wind has on club selection as the course has a different character from one day to the next.

Despite its stature, however, the course is by no means a no-go area for the average golfer. Visiting parties are more that welcome as are casual visitors, who often make the pilgrimage when other courses which do not benefit from the links' natural drainage are out of commission.

FACTFILE

Address: Seaton Carew Golf Club, Tees Road, Seaton Carew, Hartlepool.

Telephone: (01429) 266249

Course: Old course: 6,604 yards; Brabazon course: 6,849 yards

Par: Old course: 72; Brabazon course: 73

Green Fees: Weekdays £24 day; weekends £32 day

Special deals: On application to the hon. secretary.

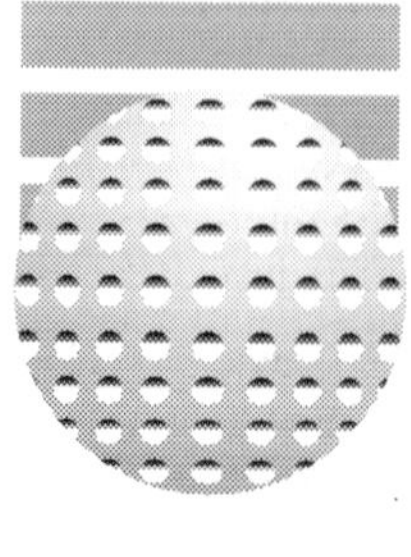

Middlesbrough Municipal

Middlesbrough Municipal is one of the busiest courses in Europe with over 65,000 rounds played in 1993, but despite the wear and tear it endures it was ranked in the top 18national municipal courses in a recent BBC poll.

At 6,333 yards with a strict par of 71, the former Netherby Farm site stands as testament to the efforts of Middlesbrough District Council who pride themselves on offering the game to people who were hitherto prevented from playing due to long waiting lists and restrictions at private members' clubs.

The municipal has produced a number of good players from its ranks, the most notable being Alex Russell who as well as lifting the NYSD's Matchplay title, has also represented the Teesside Union on numerous occasions. The club also provided its first Teesside Union president in 1994, Geoff Moore, a reward for his unstinting work both at Middlesbrough and within the Teesside area, their six-man team giving him a splendid bonus in his year of office by winning the Yorkshire Inter-District team championship just up the road at Teesside.

The course is well balanced with four par 3s and three par 5s the closing hole being in the latter category and appears for all the world as a gift of a closing birdie on paper at 481 yards.

However, a tight drive and out-of-bounds ever present down the right ensures that discretion be the better part of valour for the rank and file. The pick of the par 4s are the fourth and fifth, both in excess of 400 yards. Accuracy off the tee as elsewhere on the course is paramount to avoid the numerous strategically placed fairway bunkers ready to catch the errant drive. The toughest of the par 3s is the 11th at 206 yards only the sweetest struck wood or long iron is likely to yield regulation figures.

Middlesbrough Municipal's finest hour came in 1981 when they hosts one of the area's top pro-am tournaments, the Hintons Cleveland Charities Classic which attracted some of the leading names in the golfing world including Tony Jacklin, Sandy Lyle and Mark James.

The club house at the Muni, as it is affectionately known, is open to the public and provides an excellent opportunity for golfers and non-golfers alike to relax side by side with a varied calendar of social functions. The driving range and golf shop are an added bonus at this truly cosmopolitan club which has been used as a blueprint for many new pay as you play courses in the area and further afield.

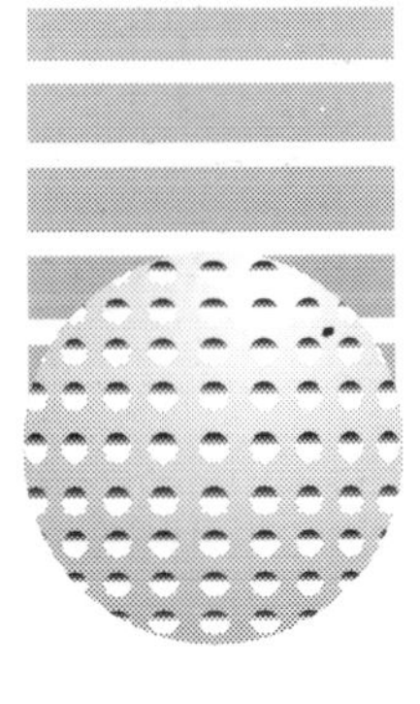

VALUE FOR MONEY
3-DAY GOLF SCHOOLS - £135.00

including 2 Nights Bed and Breakfast

DATES AVAILABLE ALL YEAR ROUND

Contact Andrew at

Hunley Hall Golf Club,
Brotton, Saltburn-by-the-Sea, Cleveland TS12 2PP
Tel. and Fax (01287) 77444

GB18

HUNLEY HALL GOLF CLUB
No. 1 For Your Day Out

Visiting Parties or Company Days

We can cater for all your needs from 10-110 people

Packages start from £22.00

to include your golf, use of driving range, coffee and biscuits and your evening meal in our Cattersty Restaurant

Contact Andrew on

(01287) 77444 or Liz **(01287) 76216**

Crossing the river at the 6th on Durham City golf course

The 1st green at Barnard Castle Golf Club

GOLF COMPLEX

18 Hole Public Course

COURSE OPENING TIMES

Weekdays 7.00 a.m.-8.30 p.m. Weekends 7.00 a.m.-6.30 p.m.
Driving Range Open Daily 7 a.m. to 9 p.m.

DRIVING RANGE

Buckets £2.00 & £1.75 Club Hire £1.50

GREEN FEES

Weekdays £6.00 Weekends £7.00
Reduced Rate for OAPs and Under 16's Club Hire £3.50

VISITING PARTIES WELCOME

Group and Individual Lessons available from resident professional Clive Burgess

For further details contact the professional's shop on

(01325) 310820

or call in at

The Oak Leaf Golf Complex,
School Aycliffe Lane,
Newton Aycliffe

GB2

Solberge Hall Hotel

Newby Wiske, Northallerton, N. Yorkshire DL7 9ER

- ★ **Senior Citizens Lunches £6.50 (weekdays only)**
- ★ **16 Acres of private grounds**
- ★ **25 en-suite Bedrooms**
- ★ **Award winning Restaurant**
- ★ **Setting second to none**

- ★ **Wedding Receptions**
- ★ **Private Enterrtaining**
- ★ **Conference Facilities**
- ★ **Evening Meals**
- ★ **Afternoon Teas**
- ★ **Luncheons**
- ★ **Christmas and New Year Festivities**
- ★ **Discount Fees available for residents at Romanby Golf Course**

Please Contact Reception

(0609) 779191

GB32

AA Rosette

Best Western

Egon Ronay **Michelin**

Your Local Irrigation Specialists

Competitive estimates for the installation of Toro Irrigation Systems
Maintenance and Repair of all types of Irrigation Systems
Many of the club's featured in this publication benefit from our Service Contract Agreement. Details available on request

UNIT 18, CAMP HILL CLOSE, DALLAMIRES LANE, RIPON, NORTH YORKSHIRE HG4 1TT

Telephone Ripon (01765) 602175

Fax. Ripon (01765) 603488

TORO

A Member of The British Turf Irrigation Association

Directors: E. B. & L. Sims Registered No 2643381 VAT Reg No 362 0003 13

GB29

NORTH YORKSHIRE

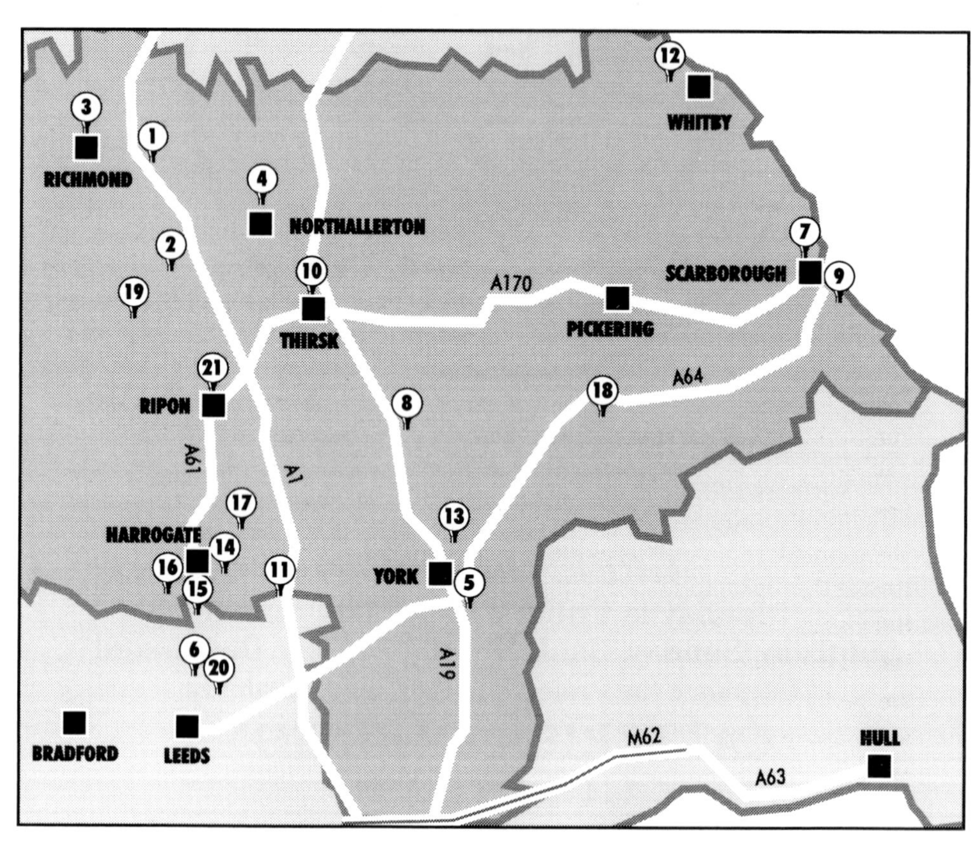

1 Catterick
2 Bedale
3 Richmond
4 Romanby, Northallerton
5 Fulford, York
6 Alwoodley
7 Ganton, Scarborough
8 Easingwold
9 Scarborough
10 Thirsk
11 Wetherby
12 Whitby
13 Strensall, York
14 Harrogate
15 Pannal, Harrogate
16 Oakdale, Harrogate
17 Knaresborough
18 Malton
19 Masham
20 Moor Allerton
21 Ripon

North Yorkshire courses

Catterick Golf Club

THE approach to Catterick Golf Club gives the impression that the challenge in store may resemble one of the disciplines in TV's Krypton Factor.

But after emerging from the garrison, visitors are plunged straight into a tranquil setting which houses a surprisingly attractive and demanding course. Some of the holes do require a degree of climbing but, mercifully, the two most prolonged ascents are in the first three holes, when hopefully the legs are fresh enough to cope.

Also, the view across the Yorkshire Dales to the west and to Cleveland and the Tees estuary to the east, makes the effort well worthwhile. The first three holes are also worthy of note because of their influence on the scorecard.

The first, an uphill 410-yard par four, is one of the most difficult opening holes in the North-East. The fairway is generous enough, although out of bounds away to the right does await the more wayward loosener. Even the most sweetly-struck tee-shot will require at best a long iron for the second, and the fairway tightens to a bottleneck 60 yards short of the green. A glance at the hole's name, Stalag, when recording your eventual number sums up the hole neatly.

The second is a classic southpaw dogleg which, with its contours throwing a tee-shot towards the angle, offers the temptation to cut off more than is prudent. Again only a confident strike from the tee affords a view of the green, a deceptive 150 yards from the corner.

The third, dubbed Heartbreak Hill, is another demanding par four. With gorse and the out of bounds fence separating the fairway from the military road on the right, there is a temptation to thumb down a passing Chieftain and ask for a lift to the next tee.

The art is in consolidation on the initial holes as there are several birdie opportunities coming up. The ninth is an excellent par four from an elevated tee, with out of bounds down the right and trees blocking the route to the green for anything struck left.

The second to a kidney-shaped plateau green, with a deep bunker eating into the front left, has precious little at the back to give an accurate perception of length and makes this hole a little gem. The tenth is another good hole, with the big hollow in front of the green

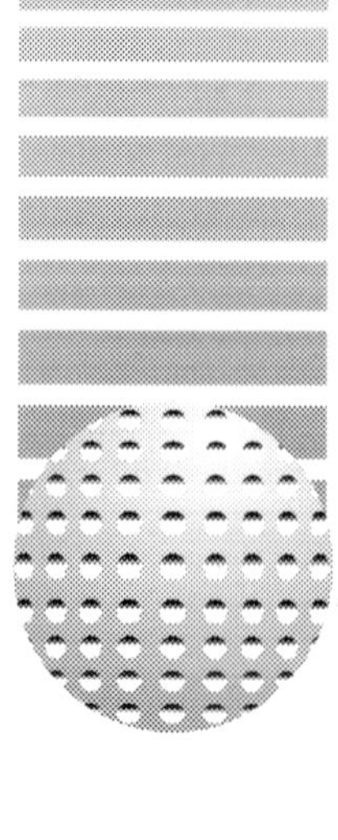

Catterick Golf Course

catching even the big hitters' tee-shots since the hole was lengthened on the advice of the late Fred Daly, famous as the only Irishman to win the Open.

As president of the Green Howards Golf Society, Fred was a regular visitor to their annual open at Catterick. After his death the Green Howards made a contribution to the club to fund the building of the new tenth tee.

Another welcome alteration was the removal of the wall which separated the halves of the course. The stones have been used to create a number of bridges throughout the course.

The 14th and 15th, both tough par fours, are the back nine's answer to the opening holes and make score protection very difficult. The 16th and 17th afford a slight respite, but the final hole, dubbed Devil's Elbow, provides a fitting climax.

The club was formed in 1930 by General Sir Walter Kirke, and it has been said that it was the best order he ever made. The officers' club was

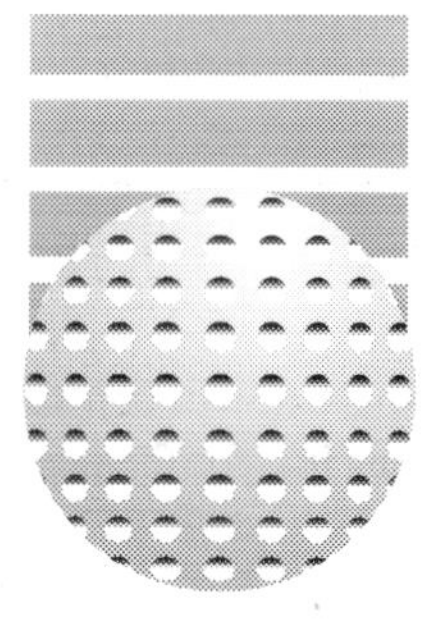

Catterick Golf Club

made available to golfers, being adjacent to the first and 18th holes.

The club moved to its current site in 1938 to accommodate the extension of membership to all ranks. It was opened officially by the staging of an exhibition match between four well-known professionals, including Peter Alliss's father, Ryder Cup player Percy Alliss. It was not long before civilians were admitted and today the balance is two to one in favour of civilian membership.

Catterick is home to one of the most talented amateurs the North-East has seen, Roger Roper, a former joint winner of the English strokeplay title. Despite the demands of the family caravan business, Roger has represented England and tirelessly turns out for Yorkshire as well as the Teesside Union.

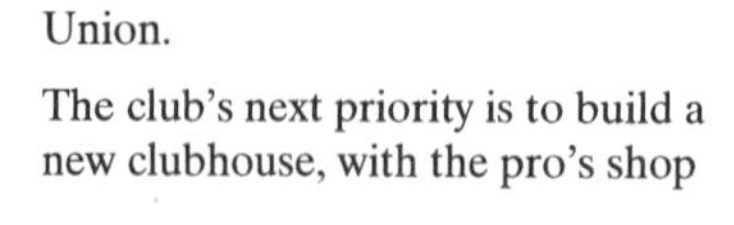

The club's next priority is to build a new clubhouse, with the pro's shop being the one of the first considerations. This is welcome news for professional Andy Marshall, who, since his move from Thirsk and Northallerton, has added his own blend of enthusiasm.

Andy is one of the new breed of club professionals not content to sit back and expect members automatically to patronise his shop. He has even coined his own catchphrase 'let's do a deal,' inviting members and visitors to give him an opporunity to compete on price with high street or mail order equipment companies. Catterick provides an excellent workout for golfers of all categories and a visit will certainly leave you well fulfilled.

FACTFILE

Address: Catterick Garrison Golf Club, Leyburn Road, Catterick Garrison, North Yorkshire.

Telephone: (01748) 833268

How to get there: Six miles south of Scotch Corner, turn off A1 at Catterick Garrison and follow signs for two and a half miles

Green Fees: Weekdays £20; weekends £25

Course length: 6,313

SSS: 70

Special deals: Societies by appointment.

Other information: Present clubhouse to be replaced.

Fulford Golf Club

Fulford, situated close to the Minster city's university, is probably the most familiar to northern golfing spectators having until recently hosted the region's only regular European tour event the Benson and Hedges International.

Many tournament starved devotees made the annual pilgrimage to the York club but scarcely got an insight into the demands required of the club golfer on the testing parkland course as the professionals more often than not reduced the 6,775 yard par 72 layout into a sub-par extravaganza.

The course is a fine example of the flair used by renowned architect Dr Alister Mackenzie creating what is one of the least physically demanding courses in the area but demands a supreme test of mental agility.

Using the natural parkland location the course weaves its way through an abundance of mature trees which line the lush fairways.

Sadly the poplars which once flanked the first hole have had to be cropped however the degree of difficulty of this most unforgiving of openers has not been affected and a par four on the 412-yarder is considered a bonus at the best of times.

Regulation figures are also welcome on the 438-yard second hole where a large fairway bunker is eager to catch the pulled drive.

A long iron par three awaits at the third followed by a 460-yard two-shotter leaving many handicap golfers punch-drunk before having a chance to unleash their Sunday best.

The fifth and ninth give an opportunity to steal something back from the course although they lie at the two ends of the par five spectrum at 561 yards and 486 yards respectively.

The second half gets under way with a classic par three where club selection is paramount, bunkers guard a tricky putting surface another unmistakeable Mackenzie trait.

On a well-balanced course the 13th provides the toughest back nine test at 473 yards, the monster par four being only seven paces shorter than its par five 18th counterpart.

The 175-yard 14th is a novel short hole capable of ruining even the best cards as a stream and bushes protect the putting surface and selection of the wrong club here makes the following trio of par fours take on an even more daunting flavour.

The 17th seems almost benign on paper at 356 yards although as with so many holes at Fulford, the combi-

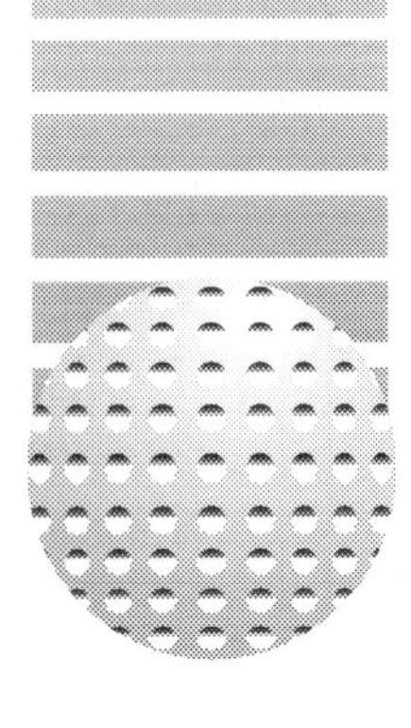

Fulford Golf Club

The 18th at Fulford

nation of maturing silver birches set among more substantial species demands the deftest of accuracy off the tee.

The green nestles in a stadium of mature trees, one of which bears a plaque commemorating one of golf's legendary shots.

FACTFILE

Address: Heslington, Lane, Heslingotn, York, YO1 5DY

Telephone: (01904) 413579

How to get there: Off A19 from York, follow the signs to University

Course length: 6779 yards

Green fees: On application

SSS: 72

As with Gene Sarazen's hole in one at the "postage stamp' at Troon, Jack Nicklaus' removal of his sweater to drive the 18th at St Andrew's, Bernhard Langer's exploits in shinning up a spreading oak and subsequently chipping his ball onto the green from the forked branches where it had finished after his approach shot will live in the memory for many a golfing generation.

And so to the final hole as previously mentioned an infinitely reachable par five by the single figure men, the performance of Ryder Cup player Peter Baker in making an eagle to force a play-off against the redoubtable Nick Faldo and duplicating the feat in the subsequent head-to-head added yet another page to the anecdotal heritage of this well-loved East Riding course.

Knaresborough Golf Club

Address: Boroughbridge Road, Knaresborough, North Yorks.

Telephone: (01423) 862690

How to get there: On A6055 (Boroughbridge road) two miles north of Knaresborough.

Course: 6,481 yards, 18 holes

SSS: 70

Special features: Parkland with minimal rough. Extensive tree plantations, 627 yards par 5 17th is one of the longest par fives in Europe (553 yards of yellow tees).

Founded: 1920

Visitors: Welcome Mon, Wed, Thurs, Fri from 9.30am, Tues from 11am, Sat and Sun 10-12 and from 2pm onwards.

Green fees: Weekday £18 a round, £24 a day; weekend £24 round £29 a day.

Hotels: Nidd Hall, Dower House, Newton House.

Further information: Prior booking for parties of 12 or more is strongly recommended. Course modified June 1994 including new long 17th. Clubhouse, major improvements planned late 1994 to early 1995.

Masham Golf Club

Address: Burnholme, Swinton Road, Masham, Ripon.

Telephone: (01765) 689379

How to get there: Leave A6108 as it skirts Masham. Go through town and towards Grewelthorpe turn right down Swinton Terrace.

Course: 5,308 yards, 9 holes

SSS: 66

Special features: Parkland. River Burn is a feature of several holes.

Founded: 1895.

Visitors: Welcome Mon-Fri

Green fees: Weekday £15; weekend N/A

Further information: Course being extended but this will only lengthen the existing course and still retain nine holes. Celebrating centenary in 1995.

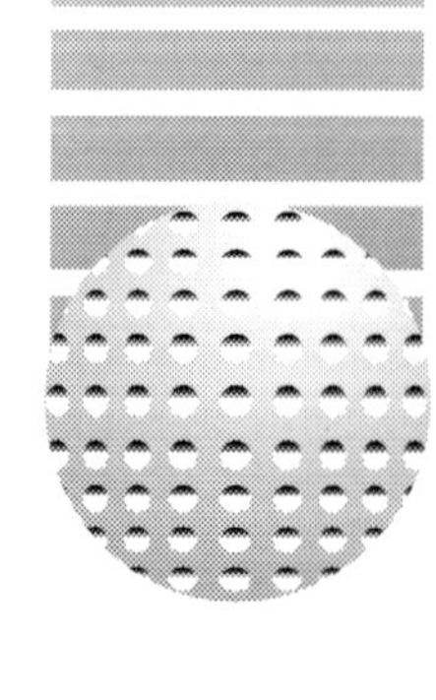

The 5th green at Ganton

The 17th at Fulford Golf Club

Bedale Golf Club

BEDALE is no longer that canny little course you pass on the way to Wetherby.

What was once a 5,600-yard pleasant stroll in the park has been transformed into a 6,650-yard test, while losing none of the inherited beauty of its deer park setting.

The club is no stranger to change. The centenary brochure outlines the various sites on which golf has been played in this gateway to the dales since the club was founded on November 20, 1894.

Ironically, the 30 acres purchased for the recent course extension were on the site of the club's third move in 1921. The members of the day remained there for just over ten years before shifting a mile away off Firby Road, where they remained until 1967.

The newly-purchased land, which cost the club about £90,000, has been used to create four new holes (11th-14th), the highlight being the 391-yard 13th, which is played from an elevated tee with a carry over area of marshland designated as a lateral water hazard with out of bounds lurking to the right.

The contoured fairway offers a reasonably generous bail-out to the left. But big hitters will fancy their chances of making the 200-yard carry to the safety of the flattened wider fairway which, against the wind, leaves a tricky approach shot to a sharply sloping two tiered green.

The club commissioned F W Hawtree and Sons, golf course architects since 1912, to propose the new layout, which has meant alterations to nine holes. Where there used to be six par threes there are now only three, and 25 new bunkers have been built.

The old 14th and 15th, previously par threes, have been combined to make a 427-yard dog-leg, while the eighth has been extended by 100 yards and a new 15th green has been constructed above and to the left of the original.

Central to all the activity is course manager Gary Munroe, who is very much one of the new breed of forward-thinking enthusiasts.

He has recently been elected secretary of the Cleveland section of BIGGA, the greenkeepers' association. Gary has worked closely with Simon Gidman of Hawtree's and they have carried out the Hawtree philosophy of 'suiting the golf course to the site, not the site to a preconceived idea of what a golf course should be.'

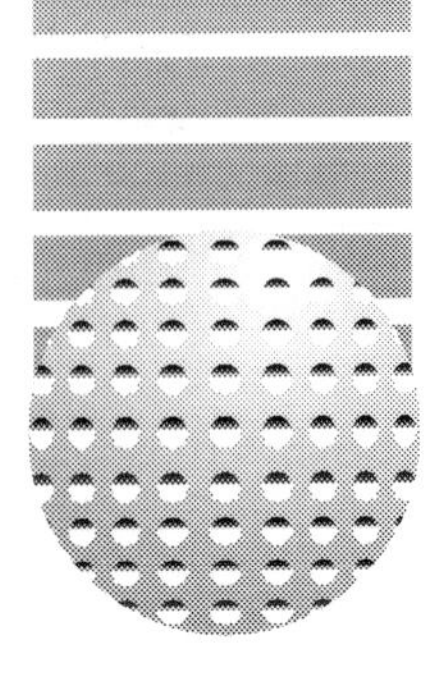

Bedale Golf Course

'I am really enjoying the challenge,' remarked the jovial son of former Eaglescliffe professional Jim Munroe (who may have considered disowning him had he seen him inadvertently redesign the tee marker with his drive at the second hole on our visit).

'To improve a course as beautiful as this and transform it into one of the best in the area is very gratifying. It would be nice to think we could host a top Yorkshire county event once the new holes have matured.'

Some of the course's magnificent trees are believed to be over 300 years old. The two superb specimens which flank the third fairway leave little margin for error and help to make it an excellent hole. Trying to play a shot round them should you stray is almost futile.

The tenth hole also owes its individuality to a menacing oak which

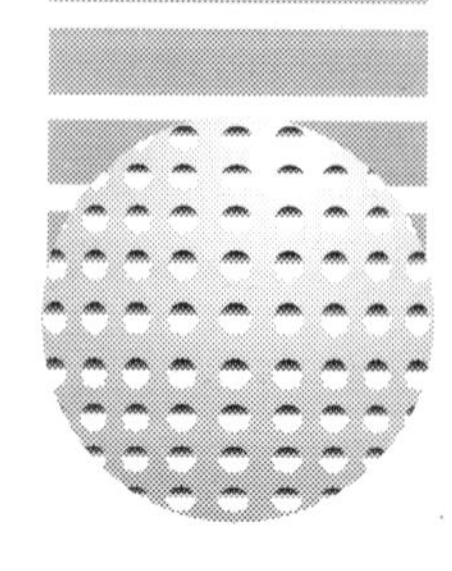

bisects the fairway. An accurate drive is a must here, yet the view from the tee gives the impression of complete freedom, such is the subtle attraction of this 521-yard par five.

The club has not restricted its forward-thinking to the course. The building of a two-tiered clubhouse in 1976 was followed by an extension in 1989.

The lounge affords an excellent vantage point for half a dozen holes and is the perfect place to watch the sun setting over the dales.

Former captain John Walker is the man behind the centenary brochure, which took three years to compile. The centenary committee unearthed a number of interesting points, including the fact that The Reveller, a famous 19th century racehorse, was buried on the site which is now the 15th tee.

The club also hosted a charity exhibition match in 1947 for the Services Benevolent Fund, which saw four of the leading professionals of the time, Norman Van Leeder, Bobby Locke, Syd Scott and Bill Shankland, testing their skills over the course.

The centenary captains were nominated as Alistair Bullen and Beth McCash. It is hoped Mr Bullen does not receive too much ribbing from the members, who may recall him turning up at 5pm at Masham for a rabbits' match when he was captain of their section, to stand on the first tee for what seemed an age before realising he should have been at Bedale.

He rushed back and played his match ...... then realised he had left his suit hanging in Masham's locker room.

FACTFILE

Address: Bedale Golf Club, Leyburn Road, Bedale, North Yorkshire.

Telephone: (01677) 422451 422568

How to get there: On A684 immediately on leaving Bedale

Green Fees: Weekdays £18; weekends £28

Course length: 5,599 yards

SSS: 68

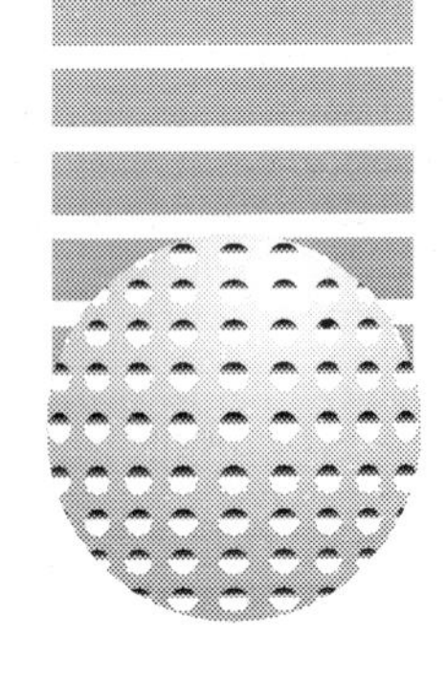

Richmond Golf Club

THERE are two Richmond Golf Clubs. One in North Yorkshire and one in Surrey. Both have 18 holes and there the similarity ends.

The Surrey version charges an entry fee of £1,000 and an annual fee of £750, compared with £247 in both cases in North Yorkshire, with green fees of £38 and £16 respectively.

At Richmond, Surrey, lady members are not allowed; in North Yorkshire there are three ladies on the management committee.

The golf boom began rather earlier in London, so much so that Richmond, Surrey, has had a membership waiting list for more than ten years. Richmond, North Yorkshire, doubled its overall membership to a healthy 724 by taking on 370 new members between 1989 and 1991.

Renowned for its picturesque setting, it has the reputation of being a friendly club, both on and off the course. At 5,769 yards it presents no great demands as a test of golf, although it is only 200 yards shorter than its counterpart in Surrey.

Established in 1892, the North Yorkshire club was originally sited at Nestfields before moving on to the racecourse, then to its current site at Bend Hagg around 1904. Its purpose was as a nine-hole recreation for the landed gentry and officers of the locally-based Green Howards until after the Second World War.

Members cut the fairways and greens as well as making small alterations, a tradition which has been maintained on a more modest scale to the present day.

An unusual feature of the course is that the first hole is possibly the best. A par five, it offers big hitters the option of going for the green with their second over the corner of a rocky outcrop, where bushes and heavy rough will gobble up a wayward shot.

The more conservative approach is through the narrow gap between the rocky outcrop and the out of bounds field on the left, leaving a short pitch to the green. The next two are both short par fours where hookers are guaranteed an attack of the jitters.

This applies particularly at the third, where there is no margin for error up the left because of an out of bounds area.

The natural tendency to aim right on this hole greatly endangered people putting on the fourth until a new green was built a couple of years ago.

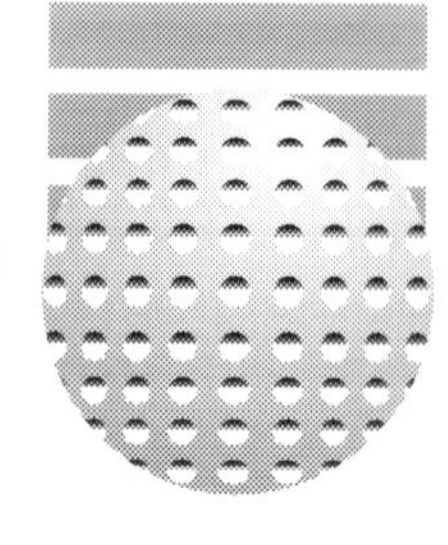

Rainy day golfing

The 512-yard sixth straddles a valley which features on several holes, notably the two most difficult par fours, the eighth and 15th. Following elevated tee-shots these two holes are mostly uphill and require good strikes to get home in two.

Otherwise most of the par fours are in the drive-and-flick category and the par threes are more likely to live in the memory.

The construction of a new tee at the seventh means a carry of 190 yards is required over a small valley. The tee is close to the fence separating the course from the Zetland estate, so again anything pulled left is out of bounds.

The ninth is another attractive par three through a heavily-wooded area to a green set in the foot of the bank leading back up to the clubhouse. The 12th is a mere 138 yards, but a menacing bunker awaits anything short, while the final par three is the notorious 18th. This involved a 170-yard blind shot over a tree-filled quarry until a gap was bulldozed through the trees.

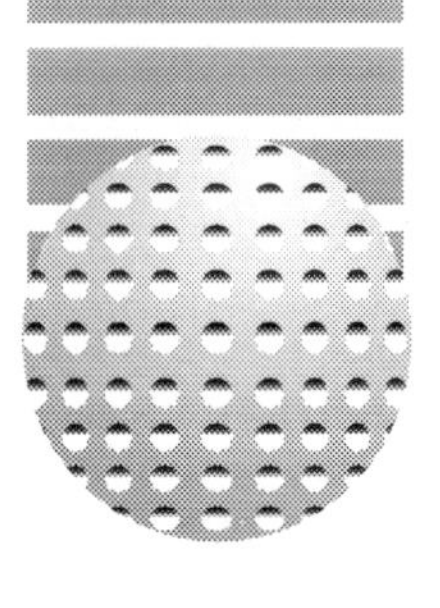

Richmond Golf Club

The first professional and greenkeeper was Harold Webster, who joined the club in 1923. Uncle of BBC commentator Clive Clark, Harold spread his workload between Richmond and Catterick and, like current professional Paul Jackson, was a left-hander.

He retired in 1972 and it was at this time that the club decided to extend the course to 18 holes, commissioning Frank Pennink to design the layout.

Once the course was finished attention was focussed on the clubhouse, with the foundation of today's impressive 19th hole being built with an excellent vantage point overlooking the infamous 18th green.

The club had lived very much from hand to mouth throughout its existence, a section of the minutes showing that a deposit for the return of a gas bottle back in the 1930s would allow payment of the greenkeeper and his lad.

FACTFILE

Address: Richmond Golf Club, Bend Hagg, Richmond, North Yorkshire.

Telephone: Clubhouse (01748) 824308; pro shop (01748) 822457; secretary (01748) 823231.

How to get there: Take A6108 from Scotch corner, turn right at traffic lights after four miles

Green Fees: weekdays £16; weekends £25

Course length: 6,262

SSS: 68

Special deals: Full days golf, coffee, lunch, three course meal for £25

However, the course began to attract more and more fee-paying visitors in the mid-Eighties, which prompted the club to advertise membership aggressively providing a much-needed injection of cash.

The clubhouse has had a series of extensions, the most recent creating an impressive conservatory-type area which looks over the course.

Richmond's fresh approach to club golf augurs well as they begin their second century and with a course which continues to improve, the future looks very bright.

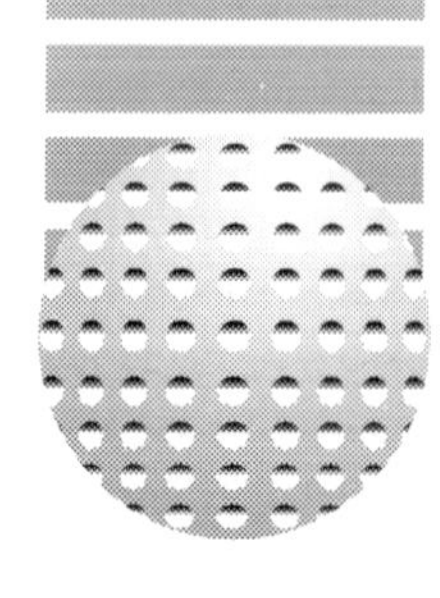

Thirsk and Northallerton Golf Club

Address: Thornton-le-Street, Thirsk.

Telephone: (01845) 522170

How to get there: On Thirsk to Northallerton road, a quarter of a mile from A19.

Course: 6,342 yards, 9 holes

SSS: 70

Special features: Parkland

Founded: 1915

Visitors: Telephone before arriving Mon, Tues, Thurs, Fri.

Green fees: Weekday £15 a round, £20 a day.

Further information: No catering on a Tuesday.

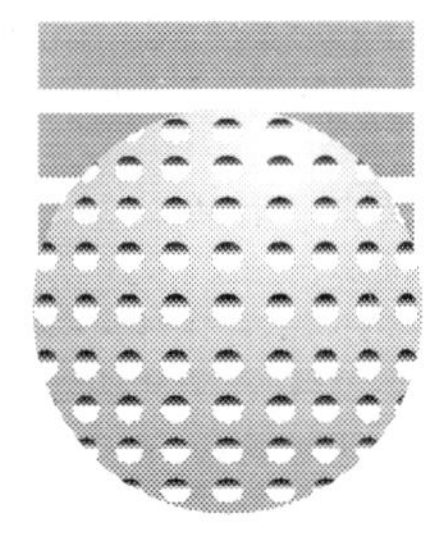

Romanby Golf Club

ROMANBY golf course, on the outskirts of Northallerton, is one of the most exciting to be built in the area for many years.

Set in natural undulating terrain, several holes are played around the meandering River Wiske while the architect, Will Adamson, has constructed two-and-a-half acres of man-made lakes to complement the 6,500-yard layout, water coming into play on no fewer than seven holes.

The course was the vision of owner Brian Craven's father, who, after farming the land as a tenant, bought it in 1957.

Unfortunately, he died before seeing his dream come to fruition. However, Brian, his mother Gladys and wife Julie have dedicated themselves to the task of creating a fitting monument, one which was made possible by a chance meeting with a Dutch consortium who were so impressed by the idea that they took a 50 per cent share, making a significant cash injection helping to get the project off the ground.

Planning permission was granted in 1989 and with help from the Agricultural Advisory Commission (ADAS) the blueprint for the magnificent course was drawn up and included the planting of 38 acres of trees, all indigenous English species.

A purpose-built driving range was opened in 1992 which attracted many visitors and gave the complex a source of income while building work got underway.

It was at this time that Fred Thorpe, a well known professional who served eight years at Catterick Garrison and 16 years at Stressholme, Darlington's municipal course, moved to Romanby.

'It took a lot to make the move, but as soon as I saw the layout of the course and the surrounding countryside, it was the beginning of a love affair,' said the PGA professional.

The eight green staff headed by Robert Upton, the course manager, formerly of Cleveland, carried out the construction programme which included the building of the greens to USGA standards with ample teeing areas on all holes.

The course has received nothing but praise from those who have taken the opportunity to pit their golfing wits against the excellent challenge the layout presents.

Although the course is ostensibly pay-as-you-play, 300 memberships were made available.

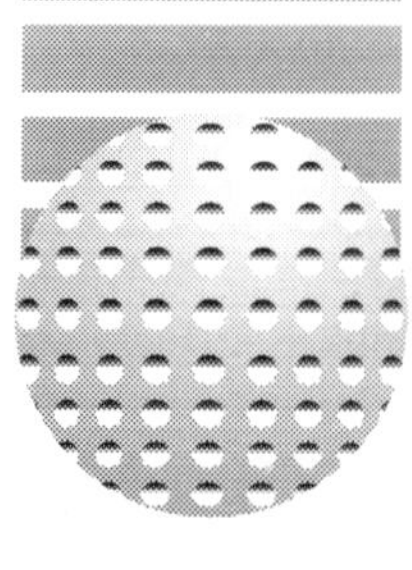

Romanby Golf Club

The 18th at Romanby Golf Club

Hole 1 is a 335 yards par 4 – a gentle opener with banking on either side of the fairway, the second shot is to a receptive kidney-shaped green.

You move on to a 382 yards par 4 which is the first introduction to the lake which crosses in front of the putting surface, making the second shot a real challenge. There is a 'bail out' area to the left of the green with the option to lay-up.

Hole 3 is a really good two-shotter with fairway bunkers flanking the landing area. The elevated green is also guarded by two sand bunkers.

There is a subtly contoured green guarding three awaiting bunkers on hole 4 and then there's a major test at hole 5 which has its own lake guarding the sliced tee shot.

You get a slight respite at hole 6 and the next is a birdieable par 4. Hole 8

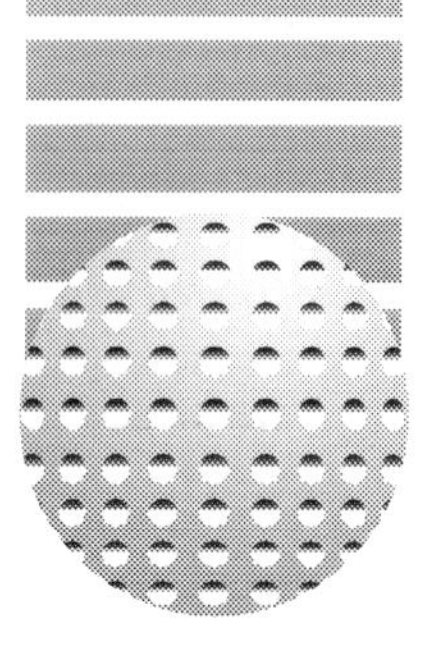

is a classic par 3 played to a slightly elevated green. Yafforth All Saints' Church gives an excellent backdrop to a green protected by a mature ash tree to the rear left.

Hole 9 is one of the signature holes of the course (yes, there are more than one). The hole is played along the bottom of the river valley with out of bounds to the right, courtesy of the Wiske with the approach road to the left also OOB. Accuracy is paramount for both drive and second shots with the approach played to a natural amphitheatre with bank and mature trees to the rear and right.

They say 13 is unlucky for some and hole 13 can be a killer. This is a classic golf hole set in natural surroundings. A tight drive with out of bounds to the left and tree plantation to the right. The hole then dog-legs left down a steep slope where a loop of the river cuts into the front and right of the slightly elevated green.

FACTFILE

Address: Romanby Golf Club, Yafforth Road, Northallerton North Yorkshire

Telephone: (01609) 779988

Course length: 6,663

Par: 72

Green fees: £10.50 per round and £15 per day weekdays, £14 per round £21 per day weekends

Special packages: May be available.

There's a chance of clawback at hole 16, a par 5, 563-yarder, which is not quite as formidable as the rest of the back half, always supposing you avoid some very strategically placed bunkers!

By the time you get to the last, you find that hole 18, a 350 yards par 4, is a dramatic finishing hole with several playing options. A carry of 230 yards from the tee over the river will reduce the hole considerably.

However, the green is surrounded by the same stretch of river. The sentiment of the course is epitomised by this hole.

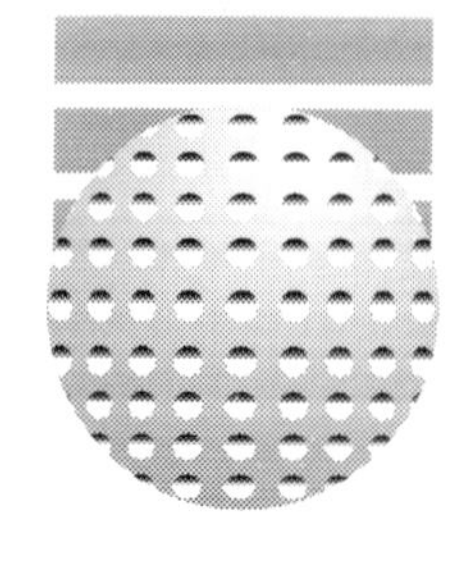

The 7th at York Golf Club, Strensall

York Golf Club

Address: Lords Moor Lane, Strensall, York.

Telephone: (01904) 490304

How to get there: Two miles north of York on A1237 exit Strensall.

Course: 6,302 yards, 18 holes

SSS: 70

Special features: Heathland. Seventh pond hole at 156 yards. The pond attracts many balls.

Founded: 1890.

Visitors: Welcome Monday to Friday and Sundays for parties.

Green fees: Weekday £20 round, £26 per day; weekend £32.

Further information: A very attractive flat and testing course.

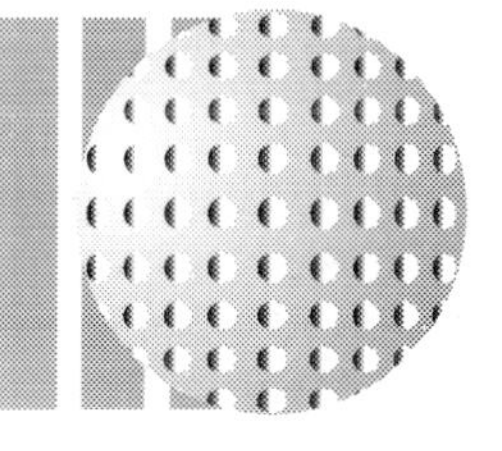

Alwoodley Golf Club

Alwoodley lies in the Leeds golden triangle of golf sandwiched between Moortown and the resited Moore Allerton course.

On striding the wonderful course and tree-lined fairways it is difficult to believe that the bustling city centre is five minutes drive away. The picturesque club was for a number of years the adopted home of the former secretary Dr Alistair McKenzie who went on to become one of the game's most respected course architects.

His greatest achievement was the design in conjunction with Bobby Jones of the Augusta National – perennial venue of the US Masters. Indeed it was a visit to the club around the turn of the century by Harry S Coat who himself created such masterpieces as Wentworth and Brancepeth Castle who viewed some of McKenzie's plans for alterations to the course at Alwoodley and set the Scottish doctor on a voyage of architectural creativity.

The opening two holes give little indication of what lies ahead, provided the out of bounds is avoided off the first tee, with the following quartet of tough par fours all too eager to take their toll on the scorecard. The first par five gives scant respite at 543 yards with trees down the left acting as a magnet for the happy hooker who is also likely to have difficulty negotiating the dog leg tenth whose green nestles in a blind hollow.

It is the finishing stretch which frustrates the golfer knowing that despite what has gone before the trio of 400 yard plus par fours must be negotiated before reaching the sanctuary of the beautifully appointed clubhouse.

Allwoodley is an exclusive club, of that there is now doubt. However it is possible to play the wonderful links with a letter of introduction to the secretary.

FACTFILE

Address: Alwoodley Golf Club, Wigton Lane, Alwoodley, Leeds LS17 8SA

Telephone: (01532) 681680

How to get there: Five miles north of Leeds on the A61 Leeds to Harrogate road

Visitors: Weekdays only. By arrangement

Green Fees: Weekdays £35

Course length: 6,686 yards

SSS: 72

Other information: Bar and restaurant by arrangement

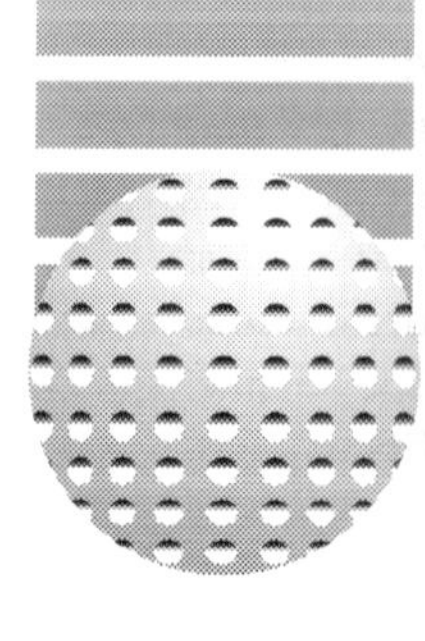

Easingwold Golf Club

Address: Stillington Road, Easingwold

Telephone: (01347) 21486

How to get there: One mile from A19 along Stillington Road. The junction is at the south end of the town.

Course length: 6,048 yards yellow, 18 holes

SSS: 70

Special features: Mainly parkland with many trees. 13 par 3 is to a sloping green fronted by an attractive pond.

Founded: 1930

Visitors: Usually unrestricted when there is no club function. Prior arrangement is advised.

Green fees: Weekday £23; weekend £28.

Further information: Society booking enquiries should addressed to the assistant secretary.

Moor Allerton Golf Club

Address: Coal Road, Wike, Leeds.

Telephone: (01532) 661154

How to get there: From Leeds city centre, distance five miles. A61 to Shadwell Village.

Course length: Lakes course 6,470 yds, Blackmoor 6,673, High 6,841. 27 holes

SSS: 71

Special features: First ever Robert Trent-Jones designed course in UK.

Founded: 1923.

Visitors: Midweek only as groups, in addition individuals on Saturdays.

Green fees: Weekday £36; weekend £50.

Special packages: On application

Hotels: Several in area

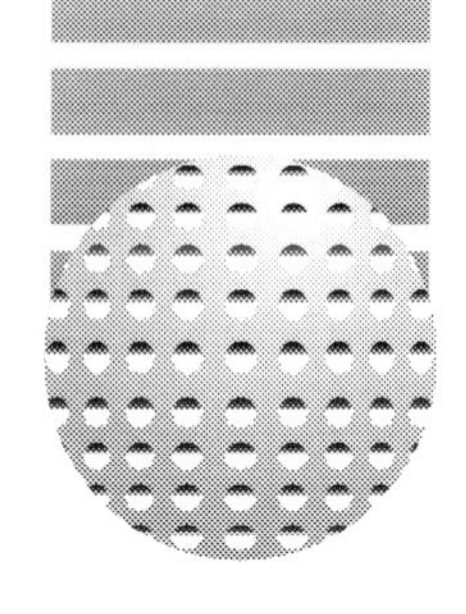

Oakdale Golf Club

Address: Oakdale, Harrogate HG1 2LN

Telephone: (01423) 567162

How to get there: From Ripon Road, Harrogate, turn into Kent Road and follow the signs to the club

Course: 18 holes, 6,456 yards

SSS: 71

Founded: 1914

Special features: Undulating parkland course with panoramic views. Designed by Dr Mackenzie

Visitors: Welcome

Green fees: On application

Special packages: Societies weekdays.

Further information: Full catering facilities except Monday lunchtime, dinner by arrangement

Harrogate Golf Club

Address: Forest Lane Head, Harrogate, HG2 7TF

Telephone: (01423) 862999

How to get there: On right off A59 two miles from Harrogate towards Knaresborough

Course: 18 holes, 6,241 yards

SSS: 69

Founded: 1892

Special features: Undulating parkland course designed by Sandy Herd

Visitors: Welcome

Green fees: On application

Further information: Societies weekdays only by arrangement, parties over 12

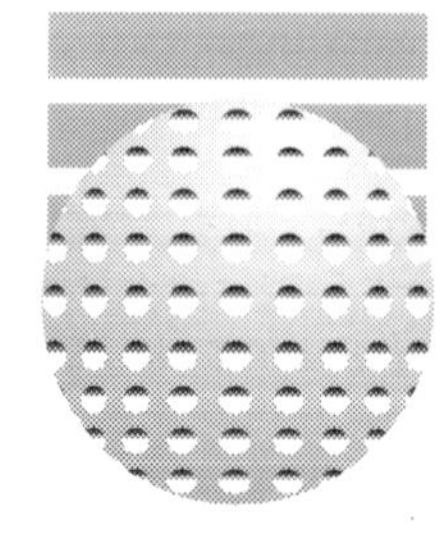

Pannal Golf Club

Address: Follifoot Road, Pannal, Harrogate HG3 1ES
Telephone: (01423) 872628
How to get there: Just off A61 Leeds Harrogate road at Pannal
Course: 18 holes, 6,659 yards,
SSS: 72
Special features: Parkland and moorland championship course designed by Sandy Herd
Founded: 1906
Visitors: Welcome weekdays
Green fees: On application
Special packages: Societies on weekdays by arrangement with the club secretary

Wetherby Golf Club

Address: Linton Lane, Linton, Wetherby.
Telephone: (01937) 63375
How to get there: From Market Place in Wetherby, turn left at La Laconda Restaurant towards Sicklinghall, 400 yards left turn golf course immediately on left.
Course: 6,235 yards, 18 holes
SSS: 70
Special features: Parkland
Founded: 1910
Visitors: Parties Mon, Wed, Thur, Fri. Independent visitors any day.
Green fees: Weekday £23 a round, £28 a day; weekend £34.
Further information: Clubhouse rebuild completed April 1994.

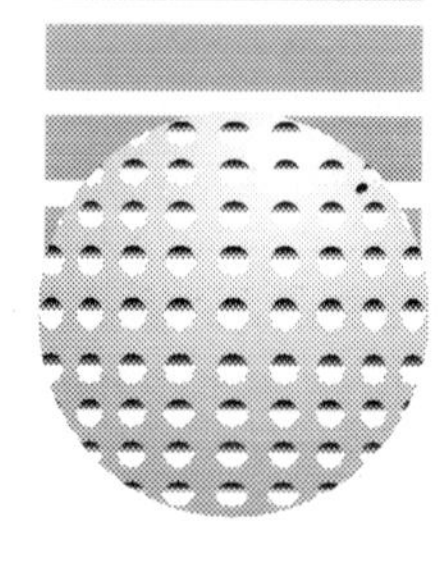

Scarborough North Cliff Golf Club

Address: North Cliff Avenue, Scarborough North Yorkshire, YO12 6PP
Telephone: (01723) 360786
How to get there: Two miles north of Scarborough on the coast road
Course: 18 holes, 6,425 yards
SSS: 71
Founded: 1928
Special features: Eleventh downhill par 3 over water to green surrounded by trees. Course designed by James Braid
Visitors: Welcome at all times except Sundays before 10.30am and on major club days. Groups of eight or more need special clearance via the club secreatary
Green fees: Weekdays £23 per day, weekends £28 per day
Further information: Clubhouse situated on cliff top overlooking North Bay and castle with views out to sea.

Malton and Norton Golf Club

Address: Welham Park, Malton, YO17 9QE
Telephone: (01653) 692959
How to get there: From the centre of Malton leave on the road signposted Pocklington Stamford Bridge. Club is on the right three quarters of a mile from the level crossing
Course: 27 holes, 6,556 yards
SSS: 71
Special features: Possibly the longest first hole in the UK. Three superb loops of nine holes, all starting and finishing close to the clubhouse!
Founded: 1910
Visitors: Welcome at all times, except during club competitions
Green fees: Weekdays £20. weekends 25
Special packages: Catering available at all times
Further information: £300,000 redevelopment of the clubhouse recently completed

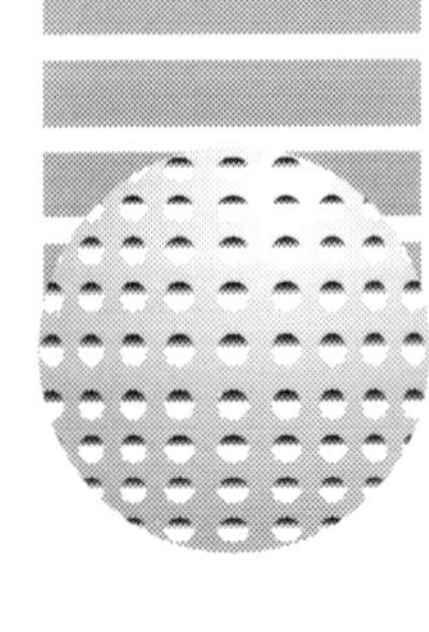

View over the 2nd green at Slaley Hall

The clubhouse at Hobson Golf Club, Burnopfield

Whitby Golf Club

Address: Sandsend Road, Whitby, North Yorkshire YO21 35R

Telephone: (01947) 602768

How to get there: Follow Saltburn to Sandsend signs on A171 between Whitby and Sandsend. Club is on clifftops coming out of Whitby into Sandsend

Course: 18 holes, 6,250 yards

SSS: 69

Founded: 1892

Special features: Drive across a ravine on the 7th hole going out and again on the 16th hole coming in.

Visitors: Welcome 8.30am to 6pm

Green fees: Weekdays £17.50, weekends £25

Special packages: Food package for £10 includes coffee and biscuits in the morning, soup and sandwich lunch and full three course evening meal

Hotels: Seacliffe and White House recommended because they are nearby

Ripon City Golf Club

Address: Palace Road, Ripon North Yorkshire, HG4 3HH

Telephone: (01765) 603640

How to get there: Two miles along the A61 Ripon to Masham road. Take the Lightwater Valley road out of Ripon

Course: 18 holes, 6,120 yards

SSS: 68

Special features: Hilly parkland. Fifth hole 165 yards carry over water to green surrounded bunkers

Founded: 1906

Visitors: Welcome any time from 8am

Green fees: Weekdays £18, weekends £25

Special packages: Coffee, lunch and evening meal

Hotels:

The Spar Hotel at Ripon and the Nags Hotel at Pickhill, Thirsk, give ten per cent discount

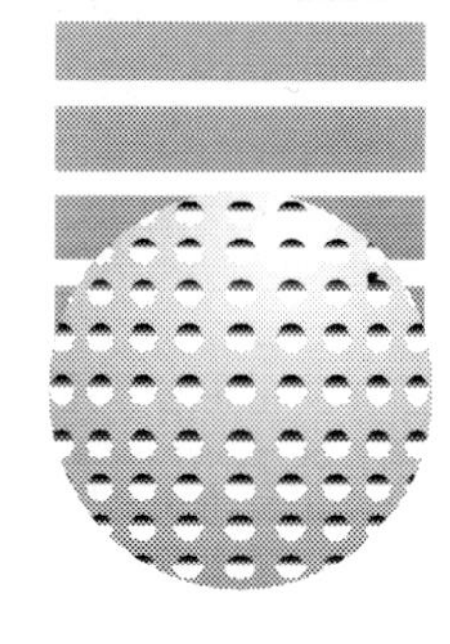

Ganton Golf Club

Ganton is one of the few North-East courses to have been afforded national recognition in an area which to many golfing scribes is considered somewhat of a wilderness.

Situated in the picturesque Vale of Pickering the inland course has many seaside characteristics but remains indelibly moorland in nature with gorse and heather flanking most fairways.

The bunkers also live predominantly in the memory of this most testing of golfing challenges, none more so than the huge sand-filled orifice which awaits the less than perfect drive from the 16th tee.

It is said you could get back-to-back coaches into the offending crater and still have room to park your car.

Ganton is a genuine championship course, a description which is much over-used in reference to newly created layouts, having staged national title events for men and women both amateur and professional for many decades.

The course has also played host to the PGA tour as recently as the 1980s. However it was as a Ryder Cup venue when first the event was played on British soil after the Second World War that its links were exposed to the unsuspecting golfing world.

Unfortunately for the club and the many keen spectators from this neck of the woods the professional game has outgrown this golfing arena with insufficient space to accommodate the huge stands which now accompany the modern tour and sadly the club must restrict its championship invitations to the amateurs.

Those taking on the Ganton experience will be surprised to note that there are but two par threes on the card, the fifth and tenth both in the middle iron category of 150-170 yards.

The opening hole demands accuracy off the tee with the aforementioned bunkers awaiting the loosener. This is followed by a trio of ample two-shotters, the most notable being the 397-yard fourth which is fraught with danger, played over a gully to a plateau green with gorse awaiting the flyer and a water hazard to the left guarding the pull.

The outward half is rounded off with an opportunity to claw a stroke back, the ninth being a par five under 500 yards. However the tee shot will examine the nerve as it is situated in a valley with trouble either side.

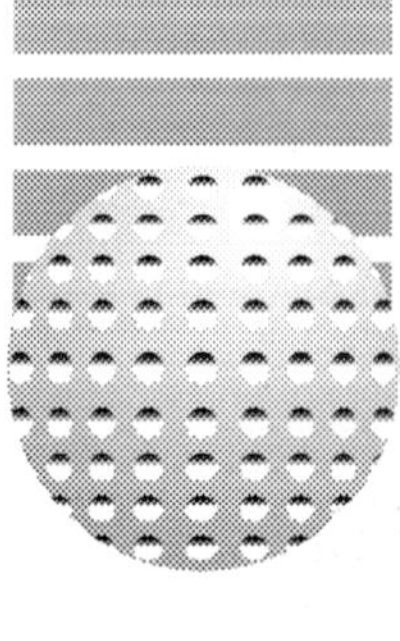

The eleventh I believe to be the pick of the bunch at little over 400 yards, this par four requires wood and fairway iron strictly out of the top drawer.

The homeward stretch has made for many exciting finishes in stroke play and match play games alike. Regulation figures likely to be accepted graciously on all but the 17th which is tantalisingly reachable provided greenside bunkers are avoided.

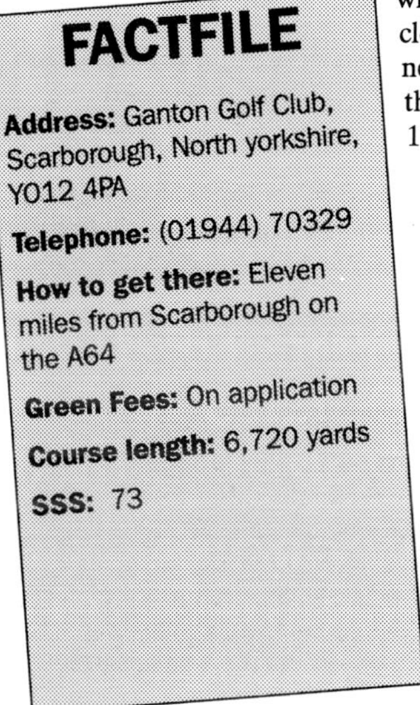

FACTFILE

Address: Ganton Golf Club, Scarborough, North yorkshire, YO12 4PA

Telephone: (01944) 70329

How to get there: Eleven miles from Scarborough on the A64

Green Fees: On application

Course length: 6,720 yards

SSS: 73

The Yorkshire club is steeped in history and the dress rules in the club (jacket and tie must be worn at all times in the lounge and dining room) continue a long tradition which stretches back to the days when the club's most famous fellow was the legendary Harry Vardon.

The six-times open champion won a hat-trick of titles when attached to the club from 1896 a record which still stands and his influence on the development of the club is still apparent today.

Reference to this wonderful course would not be complete without a mention of what has passed into the folklore of the game an amazing first round of 11 under par 61 by now secretary of the R and A Michael Bonalack in the 36-hole final of the English Amateur when he eventually closed out his opponent P D Kelley by the record margin of 12 and 11.

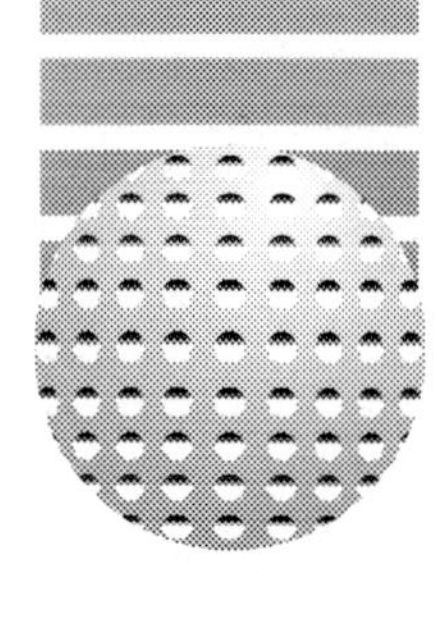

JOMAST GROUP

Delighted to be associated with local golf